AMARAVATI
PUBLICATIONS

# SIMPLE
# KINDNESS

COLLECTED DHAMMA REFLECTIONS
AJAHN CANDASIRI

Simple Kindness by Ajahn Candasiri

Amaravati Buddhist Monastery
St. Margarets Lane
Great Gaddesden
Hemel Hempstead
Hertfordshire HP1 3BZ
UK
www.amaravati.org
(0044) (0)1442 842455

ISBN: 978-1-870205-51-1

Cover and book design: Nicholas Halliday
'Northern red oak leaf' image © public-domain-image.com
Set in Gentium, Myriad Pro and Trajan

First edition, 5,000 copies, printed in Malaysia 2012

# DEDICATION

This collection of teachings is dedicated to
Venerable Ajahn Sumedho who - as a
good friend and teacher - encouraged me
to look directly at the suffering in my life,
and showed me what to do about it.

We would like to acknowledge the support of many people in the
preparation of this book, and especially the Kataññuta group of
Malaysia, Singapore and Australia for bringing it into production.

# CONTENTS

# KEY TO ABBREVIATIONS

| | |
|---|---|
| A | Anguttara Nikaya |
| M | Majjhima Nikaya |
| S | Samyutta Nikaya |
| SN | Sutta Nipata |
| Ud | Udana |

# INTRODUCTION

This small collection of teachings comprise, for the most part, talks given at a week-long retreat in Czech Republic in 2009. The final talk was given there at the New Year Retreat in 2011/2.

I presented the teachings in English, and they were translated into Czech for the benefit of the majority of retreatants who had little or no knowledge of English. This required a precision and economy of language that I found a useful discipline, once I had adjusted to the slower pace; the gaps too enabled a meditative pause - they were not, as some imagined, time to think about what to say next! My initial idea was to prepare a small book comprising transcriptions with both English and Czech side by side. It then became clear that a better approach would be to prepare and edit an English version first of all. This is what you now hold in your hands. A team of Czech translators are waiting to prepare the Czech version for publication later on.

One aim of this book is to provide an introduction for those new to the experience of being on retreat with a teacher from our Theravada tradition. The basic teachings are presented, along with supports for practice (the Refuges and Precepts); they are then returned to - sometimes two, or even three times - so that the reader, or retreatant, is constantly reminded of essential themes of practice. Please don't be surprised to encounter such topics as the Four Noble Truths, impermanence, unsatisfactoriness and non-self, or kindliness and curiosity as antidotes to the five hindrances, several times as you read through these pages.

Those with many years of contemplative Buddhist practice may also find encouragement and support in returning to these basic themes. As the teachings are applied in our lives, they work on the heart and gradually transform our view of the world so that each time we hear them something new is revealed.

More than 2500 years ago the Buddha exhorted his disciples to '... go now and wander for the welfare and happiness of many, out of compassion for the world, for the benefit, welfare and happiness of gods and humankind.' It is in this same spirit that these teachings are presented yet again.

SISTER CANDASIRI · ROCANA VIHARA · APRIL 2012.

# ACKNOWLEDGEMENTS

First to mention is Adam Long who has been a cheerful support throughout the preparation of this collection. He transcribed all the talks and, together with Pamela Kirby, ordered the material. Sash Lewis helped with editing and fine-tuning of the language.

Nicholas Halliday chose the title, and his apparently almost boundless energy is what has enabled the design and final production of the book. Talya Davies was pulled in at the last moment to give a final proofread. I'd like to express apprecation to each of them for their efforts and skill. Ajahn Amaro and Ajahn Sundara provided much needed encouragement along the way, and it was Ajahn Karuniko who kindly took time read through the entire manuscript to check that it contained nothing that would better be left unsaid.

A final acknowledgement is for Buddha Mangala, who have welcomed me to the Czech Republic over the past eight years and organised each of the retreats, for those whose skill as translators have enabled me to communicate, and for all the Czech people I have had the good fortune to meet and practise alongside.

# THE FOUR
# NOBLE TRUTHS

There's a story with which many of you are probably familiar, that begins with the Buddha walking in the woods with some of his disciples. At one point the Buddha bends down and picks up a handful of leaves from the forest floor. He holds out the leaves to his disciples and says, 'Tell me, are there more leaves on the trees and on the ground or more leaves in my hand?' His disciples say, 'There are only a very few leaves in your hand, but there are countless leaves on all the trees in the forest and on the ground.' The Buddha replies, 'Yes, that's true. The leaves on the trees and on the ground represent all the things a Perfect One can know, and the leaves in my hand represent what I teach: the things you need to know and contemplate in order to free the heart from suffering.'[1]

---

1 SN 56.31, *Simsapa Sutta (The Simsapa Leaves)*.

Some of you may enjoy speculating about where the universe began and where it's going to end, and all kinds of other questions to which there really isn't much of an answer. However, the Buddha encouraged us not to be concerned about such matters, but instead to attend to just four things. He referred to these four things as the Four Noble Truths. The first of these he called the Noble Truth of Suffering. This refers to the fact that nothing in the conditioned world can ever provide lasting peace or well-being. The effect of this is that human existence is inherently stressful.

Secondly, there is the Noble Truth of the Origin of Suffering – that there's a reason why we suffer, and we can discover it through our own observation. When we look carefully, we can notice the desire that creates a sense of unease, the wanting of things to be other than the way they are. When we attach to that desire, when we invest in it, that attachment brings a sense of stress, a sense of conflict.

The Third Noble Truth is the Truth of the Cessation of Suffering, the ending of stress or conflict. This comes about when we let go of that desire for things to be otherwise. The desire itself may still be there, but we relinquish or let go of our investment in it. We make peace with things just as they are.

The Fourth Noble Truth is the Noble Truth of the Way Leading to the Ending of Suffering: the guidelines the Buddha gave us as to how we can live our life, guidelines that can help us gradually to suffer less and less.

During the days of this retreat we'll be contemplating these truths that the Buddha presented. If we're experiencing suffering we might find ourselves thinking that we have to do something, that we have to get away from it, but the Buddha said, 'No, suffering is to be understood.' We can't possibly understand the suffering in our lives if we're constantly trying to run away from it or distracting ourselves from it. So my encouragement over these days is to really take an interest, to be curious about your lives and experience – even apparently trivial, insignificant stresses and strains and struggles, or the subtlest kinds of aversion or negativity. Take an interest in even the smallest kind of anxiety or fear, like a scientist carefully examining something under a microscope.

When I went for a walk earlier I was thinking that coming on retreat is a bit like being on holiday and making friends. That might sound surprising if you're used to the style of retreats where you are encouraged to work very hard, where the emphasis is on putting forth a lot of effort to make progress in your practice of meditation. You might also wonder what I mean by 'making friends' when we have Noble Silence, not speaking to each other unless it's really necessary. In fact, what I would like to encourage as far as possible is a sense of enjoyment, a sense of ease and relaxation. I don't mean the kind of relaxation where you just fall asleep, although some of you may experience a lot of sleepiness during the first few days. The kind of ease and relaxation I'm talking about is an alertness, a brightness, and the kind of friendship

I'm suggesting is that you try to become a bit more friendly with yourself.

One of the saddest and most difficult things for people in our Western culture seems to be their inability to actually make friends with themselves, to accept themselves as they are. We can be kind, forgiving and accepting of other people, but when we look into our own minds and how we relate to ourselves, we see that often we can be very unkind, very demanding and harsh in our judgements. So my encouragement is to get to know yourselves over these next days in a more kindly way. Notice the things about yourself that you don't like or don't approve of, and just see if you can forgive yourself for them and accept things as they are. In that way a real transformation can happen. Also, I've found that the more I make friends with myself, the more I am able to make friends with other people.

If we keep repressing the things we don't like, our unpleasant thoughts and moods, that's not really accepting ourselves and we'll probably end up getting sick. It seems that many of the sicknesses of modern times are a result of not taking proper care of our emotional life.

So we can see this time of retreat as an opportunity to do some important preventative work. If we establish an inner atmosphere of trust and kindness, our negative habits of thinking can reveal themselves. Then, having seen and acknowledged these habits, we can let them go, so that our lives need no longer be limited by their harmful effects.

# THE THREE REFUGES
# AND THE FIVE PRECEPTS

The words *Buddha, Dhamma,* and *Sangha* are used often in our practice. *Buddha* refers to the historical teacher; it also means our own capacity to wake up, to see things clearly. The *Dhamma* is the teaching the Buddha gave that points to the truth that each one of us can taste, or know for ourselves when we're fully present with things as they are. The *Sangha* is the community of the Buddha's disciples, countless generations of men and women since the time of the Buddha who have heard the teachings and, through applying them in their own lives, have been able to realize the truth for themselves and experience peace in their hearts. The word *Sangha* can also refer to a community of people who support each other in their practice, just as we are supporting each other during this time of retreat.

We call the Buddha, Dhamma, and Sangha the *Three Refuges*. These may also be called the Three Jewels, or the Triple Gem. A gem is something exquisite that can't be damaged. This is a useful simile, because we can always rely on these three refuges; they are always there wherever we go, whatever we're doing. So I encourage you to reflect on these priceless treasures, these refuges, this is how they can come to have a real meaning and value in your own lives.

The traditional supports for practice for those who choose to follow the Buddha's teaching are these three refuges, together with the Five or Eight Precepts. The Five Precepts are the ethical guidelines the Buddha recommended and encouraged for laypeople in their daily lives. The Eight Precepts are for novices or visitors to a monastery; they are also generally used as supports during a time of retreat.

The First Precept is to refrain from killing – not to take the life of any living creature, even very small creatures or creatures we don't like. We can use this precept as a guideline for ourselves. However, if we harm an insect accidentally, although it would be regrettable, it would not be breaking this Precept. The Precept simply means that we set out to refrain from intentionally harming or killing any living creature.

Secondly, we refrain from taking anything that hasn't been given to us, or made available for us to use. We don't steal from each other. This Precept is very helpful because it means that we can live together and trust each other, which is a beautiful thing.

The Third Precept is to refrain from any intentional sexual activity. When taken as one of the Five Precepts, it means refraining from sexual misconduct. We need to understand that this Precept is not a prohibition against having sexual desire – everybody naturally feels sexual desire. What we are asked to do is to refrain from acting on that desire, or, in the case of the Five Precepts, from seeking any kind of sexual gratification with someone with whom we are not in a committed relationship.

The Fourth Precept is to refrain from incorrect speech. In the context of the Five Precepts this can be interpreted as cultivating skilful speech and refraining from four kinds of harmful speech: lying, gossip or divisive speech, harsh or abusive speech and frivolous chatter. When we come on retreat we are usually asked to keep Noble Silence, to speak only when it is really necessary. This is helpful for practice, because when we keep silence externally we have a good opportunity to listen to the internal chatter of the mind. I hope that you'll also have a chance to observe how that chatter begins to die down, even just a little bit. Some of you may experience a lot of peace; for others it may be just a few moments here and there. Whether it's a lot of peace or just a little peace doesn't matter; the important thing is to notice and to be present for whatever is going on. There's no prize for the most peaceful mind!

The Fifth Precept is to refrain from taking any kind of intoxicants – alcohol or recreational drugs. If you need to take medicine that has been prescribed, that's fine - and I'm happy to say that caffeine too is allowed.

The Sixth Precept is to refrain from eating after noon, or at inappropriate times. The idea is not to use eating as a means of distraction. I remember that when I was a layperson, whenever I was feeling a bit bored or miserable I'd automatically reach out for something to eat. However, during the time of this retreat I ask you not to do that, and instead to observe whatever feeling of boredom or misery you may be experiencing – and then to notice how it changes. In that way you can have a profound insight into impermanence; you can actually observe for yourself how things change.

The Seventh Precept is refraining from entertainment, beautification and adornment. We don't wear garlands in our hair or other kinds of jewellery (wedding rings are fine), and we don't take part in sports or games, listen to music or do any of the things that are normally considered fun. Instead we have an opportunity to experience a much subtler kind of pleasure – and fun – through our meditation.

The Eighth Precept is to refrain from lying on a high or luxurious sleeping place, which might sound a bit strange. However, it is an encouragement to cultivate an attitude of wakefulness, rather than using sleep as an escape or finding pleasure through having luxurious bedding or furnishings. This doesn't mean that we can't rest or that we mustn't sleep; we just rest the body as much as is needed. We can learn so much through being awake and attentive to what's going on in our own minds and bodies.

It's important to see these Precepts as friendly supports rather than being like secret police who are going to be checking up on us, and punishing us if we make a mistake. They are available for us to use in our lives if we choose to do so. The Five Precepts remind us to keep within ethical boundaries so that, as far as possible, we avoid behaviour that is harmful to ourselves or to anyone else – behaviour that gets us into trouble. On retreat the additional renunciate Precepts support simplification. We make a conscious choice not to engage in certain activities. Through making this choice we create the space within. We can then observe directly our habitual ways of perceiving and responding to experience. Thus, we are able to see what is needed to free the heart from suffering.

# CURIOSITY AND INSIGHT

As we come to the end of the first full day of practice, it's interesting to notice the effects of this kind of effort. You may notice how different you feel now from how you felt at this time yesterday, just after you had arrived. My sense is that you are more settled, and maybe a little tired. This is normal, because I also sense that everyone has been applying a lot of effort in the meditation. Sometimes it does take a lot of effort.

This evening I would like to talk about different kinds of insight. The word 'insight' can be used to refer to *any* kind of realisation – one of those 'ahhhh' moments when you suddenly see things differently, you have a different understanding. An insight can be about quite ordinary things. As an example I'd like to tell you about a small, practical insight I had very recently. It's about the house or *kuti* where I live. I live in a very nice *kuti* that was built about fourteen years ago by one of the nuns; it's still in very good condition. However, a few years ago I began to notice that there were some creatures living in the walls and the ceiling. I wasn't sure what they were, but since we've had a bit of a problem with rats at the monastery, the people who organise the work assumed it was a rat, and decided to put wire all around the base of my *kuti*, anywhere that a rat might get in. They did a very good job ... but it was clear that the creatures were still happily there.

Trying to work out how they got in and out was a puzzle for me. In recent months they've become much more energetic, so that now it's actually quite unpleasant. At first I used to think they were rather sweet, now I find them really intrusive, so I was determined to find out how they were getting in and out so that I could do something to stop them. I thought that perhaps they were digging tunnels underneath the *kuti*, so every time I found a likely looking hole in the ground I would put a stone over it. But still they were there. Then I began to listen carefully. It sounded as though they were jumping onto the roof from the nearby trees. I asked someone to cut back the branches of the trees so they couldn't get onto the roof that way. But that didn't work either; they were still there. Then I heard that there are rats that can actually climb up the sides of buildings. I thought these must be some of those, so I took a lot of time just to look up under the roof to see if there were any holes there. But it was a well-built *kuti*, and I couldn't find any holes. Then I started looking at the tiles on the roof to see if rats could get in under the tiles, but I couldn't see any holes there either.

Eventually, in desperation, I took a stepladder so I could look properly on the roof. Then came the moment of insight: *Ahhhh!* I saw three big holes at the base of the chimney. So then, when I thought that the rats had gone out, we blocked up those holes. But that's not the end of the story, because that night there was a terrific disturbance and the sound of something chewing through the wall or the ceiling. Well, that was confirmation that the holes were how they got in *and* out. So we still haven't worked out what to do. We unblocked the holes and I'm just waiting for them to leave – and doing a chant called the snake protection chant:

*I love the no-footed creatures*
*I love the two-footed creatures*
*I love the four-footed creatures*
*I love the many-footed creatures*
*But please go away.*

I hope that gives you an idea of a moment of insight. It's when you are puzzled about something and you really investigate – and *then* you see. With our practice it's really the same principle. The Buddha's teachings are to encourage us, and to show us where to look in our own lives. We can study many books of scriptures so as to gain an intellectual understanding, but I sense that everybody here is interested in something more nourishing for the heart; otherwise you'd all be at university studying Buddhism there!

When I first heard Buddhist teachings I didn't actually realise that they were Buddhism, they just seemed like common sense - and I was very excited about the possibility of really *knowing* the truth for myself. So in coming on this retreat, we have an opportunity to contemplate the teachings in relation to our own experience. Here, the theory and the practice can come together, and when we apply ourselves there can be the arising of insight.

Something I've noticed about insight is that it often arises quite unexpectedly. We can sit or do walking meditation for hours, and nothing really seems to happen. But then, when we're doing something very ordinary like cleaning our teeth, getting dressed or going for a walk – suddenly, there is understanding. We see what was meant by a particular teaching; it becomes real for us.

Ajahn Chah told a story about an insight that he had once. He wanted to make a robe for himself. Now, our robes have a special pattern, they're sewn in a particular way which is quite complicated. So he spent the whole day thinking about it and, eventually, worked out in his mind how to make the robe. Through this experience he realised that if you're really interested in something, you naturally apply the mind to it, and in due course you naturally have the arising of insight. This is why I always emphasise and encourage an attitude of curiosity - to be curious about our experience. If we really take an interest and apply ourselves to investigating things, this is how we begin to understand.

Now, we can have insight into many things, some of which are useful from the point of view of liberation, while others are not at all useful. I think all of us here are interested in the kind of insights that will bring freedom to the heart, liberate the heart. We want to understand why we suffer. Why is there suffering? We want to understand how to free the heart from suffering. Well, we've come to the right place, because the Buddha said: 'I teach suffering, and the ending of suffering.'

I spoke yesterday about the Four Noble Truths. For each of the truths the Buddha pointed out three aspects. The first aspect of the First Noble Truth is that there is suffering. The second aspect is that suffering needs to be understood. Then comes the liberating insight that suffering *has* been understood. If we want to understand something, we need to be willing to examine it; however, this is not the normal response to suffering. Usually when there's suffering, we want to get rid of it as quickly as possible. We are not inclined to examine it. But when we follow the Buddha's way of practice, it becomes clear to us that if we want to liberate the heart from suffering, we need to examine it, we need to understand it. We can spend our whole lives trying to distract ourselves from suffering, but that doesn't get us any closer to liberating the heart.

I did my first retreat with Ajahn Sumedho about thirty years ago as a lay person. In my interview he asked me how I was getting on. I told him that I really liked the retreat, I was loving the structure of the retreat ... then I started crying and found myself saying, 'but I have all this pride. I can't get rid of these thoughts of pride!' I really thought I shouldn't have those thoughts, and I desperately wanted to get rid of them. Ajahn Sumedho and the monk sitting with him were very quiet. After a moment or two he said to me, 'It's not the *pride* that's the problem. It's the *not wanting* it.' That was an important moment for me. I clearly saw the distinction between what was happening in the mind, and my reaction to it. I could see that there was a clear distinction between the unpleasant condition and suffering. I began to see that even with unpleasant conditions of mind and body, one can in fact be quite peaceful. It became clear that the suffering was not caused by the condition itself but by the struggle to get rid of it.

Wanting things to be other than the way they are, the desire for things to be different - if we involve ourselves with that desire, it will lead us to stress, to struggle, to suffering. But if we can recognise the unpleasant condition and simply acknowledge that there is a natural desire to get rid of it, we can come to a place of real peace. This works with pleasant conditions as well. We tend to want to hold on to them, we don't want them to change, but of course they change too. So we can also suffer about pleasant conditions, if we don't really understand and accept the fact of change.

During this time of retreat we have a chance to investigate our experience, to be really curious and take an interest in our responses to the different things that arise for us. For example, some of you are not very well, you've got colds or hay fever, so you can notice the kind of negativity and aversion that arise in response to the unpleasant physical sensations – and of course the same applies for unpleasant mental conditions.

Another important aspect of insight relates to *anicca*, impermanence, change. Once I was on a walk with a group of lay people. We'd been walking for about a week through some very beautiful countryside in the north of England. One day I was standing by a waterfall, just watching the movement and patterns of the water as it fell. A poem came into my mind, which I realised, was in fact a reflection about the whole of life:

*Falling*
*Falling*
*Can you catch it?*
*Can you catch it?*
*No...*
You can't!

In our lives we sometimes experience lovely things, very beautiful things. We also have special relationships where we feel a wonderful affinity and sense of ease with certain people. There can be a desire to hold on to these experiences. But we need to realise that there is a kind of relentlessness about life. It's *anicca* - it just flows on, whether we want it to or not.

The *Dhammacakkappavattana Sutta* is the first sermon the Buddha gave after his enlightenment. In it he talks about each of the Four Noble Truths and their three aspects; there's a tremendous amount of teaching in this *sutta*. It is said that after the Buddha had presented this teaching, the Venerable Kondañña, one of the five ascetics who were listening, *understood*. The *sutta* goes on to say that he understood that, 'Everything that has the nature to arise has the nature to cease.' I love the simplicity of this. We're also told that when Venerable Kondañña realised this, all the *devas*, all the angels through all the heavenly realms were overjoyed. The earth *devas* shouted up to the next level, 'Venerable Kondañña has understood! He's got it!' and the rejoicing went right up through all the different levels of *deva* realms, and the ten thousand-fold world system shook and rocked and quaked. There was a terrific thunderstorm, and great measureless radiance pervaded the whole universe - all because of Venerable Kondañña's insight that everything that has the nature to arise has the nature to cease. Now for some of you that insight may sound like nothing much, but it was obviously extremely significant. It's something that we can contemplate over these days, so that we come to really know that everything – these bodies, these minds, the mind states, the states of the body – is continuously changing.

One of the things that I like about coming back to this retreat centre is being able to see the changes: the trees that have planted themselves in the river growing bigger, the building crumbling, noticing changes in the people I meet year after year, and seeing my own face in the mirror, seeing how it changes. For people who don't contemplate the Dhamma, watching the face change with age can be very bad news. But I quite like it.

In conclusion, the liberating insights relating to the Four Noble Truths are insights into the three characteristics of all conditions: that all things are impermanent (*anicca*), that they're all inherently unsatisfactory (*dukkha*), and that there's no permanent selfhood in anything (*anatta*). There's a phrase that I love in the morning chanting: 'For the complete understanding of this, the Blessed One in his lifetime frequently instructed his disciples in just this way.' We chant this almost every day in the monastery. I find this daily chanting helpful because it can take awhile for this teaching to really sink in.

My hope for these days of retreat is that in our meditation everyone will be able to experience some calm, some pleasant mind states, and I would also hope that everybody will have a little insight into the nature of suffering and the possibility of liberating the heart from it.

# THE FIVE
# HINDRANCES

We've been practising together for a couple of days. So far, most of the emphasis has been on meditation on calm, and I've also spoken a little about insight. Many of us, especially those who have been practising for quite some time, probably have quite a clear sense of what is needed. But although the practice is simple, it's not always easy. This is because the habits of ignorance and delusion, which have been conditioned into us ever since we were born, are very strong. We want many kinds of things, and we don't want other things. We're generally a bit confused about what's good for us, and so I'm always grateful to the Buddha for so clearly formulating the teachings and way of practice.

Many of you will be aware that in Buddhism there are many lists. This was because in the time of the Buddha the teachings were not written down. There were no recordings and people didn't take notes as we do nowadays. They gathered round the Buddha, listened to his teachings and memorised them. It seems that in those days people had very powerful memories. They could remember a terrific number of things. I think the recordings and computers and things we have nowadays have made us a bit lazy – our brains don't have that same capacity; we don't have so much memory. We're more ready to trust the memory in our computer! But in those days the Buddha's disciples would remember the teachings, and when they were travelling or away from the Buddha, they would repeat them for the people who had gathered. The teachings were passed on like this for several hundred years, before they were gathered together and written down. This seems completely mind-blowing when you see collections of the Buddha's scriptures - they contain thousands of pages and vast amounts of information.

One of the lists that I find very helpful in my practice is the Five Hindrances. This list explains very clearly why sometimes, although we know what we *should* be doing, we can't quite manage to do it. These hindrances are obstacles. They make meditation difficult for us. But when we establish mindfulness of the hindrances we can find the way through them, and then, rather than being obstacles, they can take us to a place of deeper insight, deeper understanding. So in fact they can sometimes be very useful once we've learned how to recognise them. I'll list them first and then speak a little about each one. I think you will recognise some if not all of them from your own practice.

The first hindrance on the list is sensual desire, sensual longing.
The second hindrance is ill-will, negativity, aversion.
The third hindrance is sleepiness and dullness (sloth and torpor).
The fourth hindrance is restlessness and agitation of mind; *uddhacca-kukkucca* in Pali.
The fifth hindrance is doubt.

As I said, when we recognise them clearly they are no longer hindrances, because then there are very clear ways of working with each of them. They are only obstacles when we haven't brought them fully into consciousness, when we're not really aware of what's happening. We get into trouble when we either follow them or get pulled into reacting to them. That's when they tie us up and prevent us from seeing clearly.

One of the most difficult things about the hindrances is that we can tend to complicate them by being very averse to them!

We can be upset about our greed; we feel we shouldn't be greedy, so we hate ourselves. We hate ourselves for being irritable and grumpy and negative. We can feel completely hopeless and despairing about our dullness and sleepiness. We can get totally frustrated and upset by our restless, agitated mind. And we can really struggle with doubt, not wanting it, not liking it. So we complicate these conditions still more with our aversion, our negative response to them. But when we can just recognise that this is greed, this is negativity, this is dullness, this is restlessness and agitation, or this is doubt - when we can recognise them for what they are, rather than seeing them as a problem, something we shouldn't have or some basic flaw in our character - they become an interesting puzzle or challenge, part of the game of life. They can even become fun.

Of course it's not always so easy to see them in that way. Sometimes we need a good friend to help us to look at things differently. That's one of the greatest blessings about living in a monastery. Most of the monks and nuns, particularly those who have been there for a long time, have slightly lost their sense of idealism about themselves or anybody else. They no longer expect to be perfect all the time. They're able to acknowledge and accept the hindrances. They understand that they are a natural part of the human condition; not something to be hated or feared, but something to be understood and worked with in a positive way.

At Chithurst in the very early days we all worked very hard. The house was practically a ruin, and we had to rebuild it. The garden was like a jungle. We were four novice nuns and we used to do all the cooking for everybody. Sometimes there wasn't very much to cook. We'd have beans and rice and nettles, and maybe one onion. It was lots of fun; but our meditation wasn't all that great! We'd all be sitting slumped and sleepy. I remember Ajahn Sucitto, one of the senior monks, praising and encouraging us. He said we should celebrate the fact that at least we managed to keep our heads off the floor. When you live in a community of people who practise it's possible to laugh about these things, not to take them too seriously. But when we don't have that kind of support we can feel very desperate when we experience states of greed, states of negativity or states of dullness. It can take a tremendous amount of compassion and tenderness towards ourselves to be able even to acknowledge what is going on.

I think that the reason many of us come to meditation is that we want to be a better person. But of course, as you have probably noticed, as soon as we start to meditate we become aware of all of those not-so-good things about ourselves. When I was a layperson I used to think I was a nice peaceful person. People would say, 'She's so calm. She's so placid.' But then when I became a nun I discovered this tremendous rage; sometimes I would want to hit people or wish that they didn't exist! So one cold think that maybe I shouldn't have started meditation in the first place - but I would strongly disagree. I think it's very good to meditate. We can see it as a process of inner relaxation. We're brought up to be well-behaved and good, so we learn how to push down or ignore our unpleasant qualities. Then, as we begin to meditate, we relax, and so these things begin to come to the surface. In Buddhism we talk about purifying the heart - and we do this by allowing all these things that don't seem so pure and lovely to arise. Then we can let them go. Sometimes we then discover much more energy, because we're no longer putting a lot of effort into keeping everything under control.

The Five Precepts are a protection. When we take them we refrain from killing, stealing, sexual misconduct, wrong speech or using intoxicants. They are like five good friends that remind us to be careful with the energies of desire, lust, negativity, hatred and aversion. Then, when these energies arise we can simply recognise them, and we treat them with care and respect because they can cause a lot of harm; and as we come to understand them and learn how to work with them, we're no longer afraid of them. When through our investigation it becomes obvious to us that they are *anicca*, *dukkha*, *anatta* - that they change, that they're unsatisfactory, that they're not who we are - we no longer have to identify with them, and then in a sense we're free of them. Even though they might be there we're not bound into the desire to follow them, to act on them. We have a choice.

In the scriptures the Buddha gives a number of teachings on the hindrances and different ways of working with them. He uses some very helpful similes to give a sense of what they're like and how they affect us.

Ill-will or negativity, he said, is like a disease. On retreat it's very important to look out for different kinds of negativity, particularly negativity towards ourselves. We can be very hard on ourselves, very unforgiving. We seem to be very good at seeing our faults, recognising the things that we've done wrong, but sometimes we have a real difficulty in celebrating the things that we do right. This is something to watch out for, to notice.

These hindrances can be very big, very extreme; but they can also be very subtle. Sometimes the subtler forms of negativity are more difficult to deal with. Rage is very obvious, but minor irritation or grumpiness can be more difficult to recognise at first. One of the things I've noticed in my own practice with grumpiness or irritability is that there is often the feeling that I shouldn't have them. However, now I've learned over the years to simply recognise when I'm feeling grumpy. Sometimes I even tell people, 'Don't talk to me today, I'm feeling grumpy.' And sometimes if people I know very well talk about something that upsets me, I say, 'I'm not in the mood to talk about that right now.'

So it's really helpful to recognise when there's negativity or aversion in the mind. Otherwise, it can easily escalate and affect everybody else. I remember once having a conversation with somebody about a topic in which I wasn't particularly interested, but I made some comment, and this person disagreed with me - then automatically I disagreed with her; and then she disagreed with me! and I found myself becoming more and more angry and upset. Eventually, I saw what I was doing and relaxed. I recognised that feeling of having to win an argument with somebody, and I thought, 'Actually, I don't have to do this.'

I was very impressed by a group of people working in Palestine to overcome the troubles between the Palestinians and the Israelis. Their motto is 'Peace is the most important thing.' Although this made perfect sense to me, I could see that theirs was a very demanding practice. To make peace means to give up or relinquish the position of being right. It's a real sacrifice of the ego, the sense of self; and because of the way we've been conditioned, the sense of self is *very* important to us. Even though it's only an illusion, we do everything we can to hold on to it until we realise how much trouble it causes us and everyone else.

So negativity or ill-will is like a disease.

The Buddha said that sensual desire is like being in debt, feeling that if we could only get the thing we want, we would be complete and happy. But we are *never* complete, we always want more and more, better and better - whether it's a wonderful relationship, some kind of delicious food, or a new computer, cell-phone or whatever. The Buddha encourages us to contemplate sensual desire, and consider carefully the fact that things are continuously changing. One practice that I have found useful is to contemplate delicious food *before* we eat it, and then to consider what happens *after* we eat it. It becomes less desirable, doesn't it? So as monastics we're encouraged to take food simply as a medicine, something to nourish and sustain the body. We certainly need to eat food and there's nothing wrong with that, but people can make all kinds of complications around food. I remember that at one time I was afraid that I was greedy, so I thought I should only eat a little, not realising that I was actually starving myself. Sometimes it can be difficult to separate desire for food from the need to have it as a support for bodily well-being.

Sloth and torpor are compared to being in a prison. It is as though you are in a small dark prison cell. You can't see anything outside it. You are just caught in this small space. One suggested antidote is to contemplate light. So when I feel very sleepy I find it helpful just to stare at the candle, open my eyes and look at the candle flame. Other antidotes that the Buddha recommended include pulling the earlobes, washing the face with cold water, and if everything else fails, sitting on the edge of a cliff - but I've never dared to do that!

Restlessness and agitation are compared to being a servant told to go here, go there, do this, do that, running around everywhere. Sometimes when we're worried about something the mind can become very active. Some people can be very busy; I tend to be quite busy, I like doing things. But when one is busy without mindfulness, it can create a very unpleasant energy for those around. I'm not saying we shouldn't do things, but it's much better to do them from a place of inner calm and collectedness, rather than 'running around like a headless chicken' as the expression goes. So we try to avoid doing that and to be collected and present. When we experience inner restlessness and agitation, the Buddha encourages us to focus on something calming and steadying. So my favourite antidote to restlessness and agitation is to walk on my walking path and just to be aware of the feet touching the ground, because the feet are a very long way from the head. Feet don't think.

The final hindrance is doubt, and the simile for this is being lost in the desert without a map, not knowing which way to go. I have found that one of two things happen to me when I'm not mindful of doubt. One of them is a kind of paralysis -- I don't do anything. The other is trying one thing after another - and not being sure -- trying to find an answer so as to get rid of the sense of doubt. But now mostly I don't mind doubt. Doubt can bring us to a very quiet place in the heart. When we really don't know and can *allow* ourselves not to know, it's quite peaceful. When we have a very important decision to make, if we can just allow ourselves to come to that place of not knowing, it's almost as though we allow our 'wisdom mind' to come forth. Over the years I've learned to trust the voice of the heart much more than I trust the voice of the head.

So here is a recap of the five hindrances, which as I said, don't have to be hindrances if we are conscious of them, if we are aware of them; they're only hindrances when we react to them.

Firstly, sensual desire, which is like being in debt.
Secondly, aversion or negativity, which is like a disease.
Thirdly, sloth and torpor, which is like being in prison, a small prison cell.
Fourthly, restlessness and agitation, which is like being a servant told to go here and there.
And fifthly, doubt, which is like being lost in the desert without a map.

I hope this has been helpful, and that you'll be able to be quicker to recognise any of these hindrances when they arise in your practice, instead of adding other hindrances by saying, 'I shouldn't have this. I've been practising all these years and I should have got over my rage. I'm a hopeless case because I keep falling asleep. How can I stop my mind from thinking?!? I have this terrible problem with greed.' Rather than doing that, we just recognise, 'Ah, that's just torpor.' 'Ah, that's just worry.' 'That's interesting, why do I feel so angry?' In this way we make friends with ourselves. We get to know ourselves. We take an interest in these conditions as they arise, rather than seeing them as terrible problems that turn us into a hopeless case.

We have a figure in Buddhism called Mara, who wants us to be discouraged, to think we're hopeless. Mara doesn't want us to wake up. Mara is a little like Satan in Christianity. Jesus' response to Satan is, 'Get behind me Satan.' Similarly, the Buddha's response to Mara is, 'I know you, Mara.' Poor Mara was always very discouraged when the Buddha recognised him.

# THE FOUR FOUNDATIONS OF MINDFULNESS

I want to give a bit of instruction on the Four Foundations of Mindfulness. We often talk about 'mindfulness' or 'presence'. It's not always clear how to achieve this state, though, as you'll have gathered so far, it's fundamental to the way of practice. Every time I'm asked a question or somebody comes to me to talk about a problem they're having, my immediate answer is always, 'Mindfulness.' Of course, most people's questions or problems need a bit more than that. Such an answer wouldn't be very satisfying for them! However, it's absolutely fundamental to begin by being present with what's happening here, right now – and this is the whole purpose of our meditation: to cultivate the habit of presence.

In his teaching the Buddha presented what he called the Four Foundations of Mindfulness:

*kayanupassana*: awareness of body or form
*vedananupassana*: awareness of feeling
*cittanupassana*: awareness of the mind itself
*dhammanupassana*: awareness of mind objects

They are foundations because they are basic points of reference; they're all present all of the time and they're part of our everyday experience, but our habit is to focus on other things. In a retreat situation we are reminded over and over again of these points of reference, these foundations for presence, mindfulness. Gradually, instead of believing in what passes through the mind, we become more confident in establishing mindfulness around one or more of these foundations, discovering that they are more reliable than all the ideas we have about ourselves, others, our situation and so on. Not that these ideas and concepts are all bad. Some of them can be very useful; in fact they are essential for living in community, in society, but we do need to understand them for what they are.

The body or form (*kaya*), is the first foundation of mindfulness. The Buddha uses many ways of reflecting on bodily experience. They include mindfulness of breathing or *anapanasati,* and mindfulness of posture, whether we're walking, standing, sitting, or lying down. The Buddha also spoke of mindfulness when doing the most ordinary things such as eating, drinking, bending or stretching, so that at any time of the day we can notice what the body is doing. He also encouraged an analytical approach to the body; contemplating it in terms of the four elements - seeing our own bodies as made up of earth, water, fire, and air - or reflecting on the different parts of the body. Part of the ordination ceremony for monks and nuns is drawing attention to the outward appearance of the body, the surface of the body. So each novice monk or nun repeats after the preceptor:

*kesa (hair of the head)*
*loma (hair of the body)*
*nakha (nails)*
*danta (teeth)*
*taco (skin)*

Another recitation we do in the monastery is the 'reflection on the thirty-two parts', in which we bring to mind all the different parts of the body: flesh, blood, entrails, pus ... it gets quite graphic. Now, the purpose of this practice is not to make us feel averse to or negative about our body; rather, it is useful as an antidote to strong feelings of sexual attraction. It's a way of cooling things down, but since it's a powerful practice, it needs to be used with care, preferably with the guidance of an experienced teacher who can help us to avoid developing negative feelings about the body, and instead come to a place of neutrality, of disinterest.

There's a rather strange story from the life of the Buddha about this practice. After giving a group of monks instruction on the reflection on the thirty-two parts, the Buddha went away on retreat for a couple of weeks. While he was gone many of the monks committed suicide, because they became disgusted by their own bodies and they thought they should end their lives. So the Buddha then emphasised the importance of balancing this practice, encouraging its use simply as an antidote to physical attraction that can also make us feel very peaceful.

In the same spirit the Buddha also encouraged contemplation of death, of corpses, using this too to counter-balance the tendency to become over-concerned about the body. It helps too in deepening our understanding that the body is impermanent, appreciating its limitations. I find for myself that what this does is to enhance a sense of wonder at how the body functions and survives.

So contemplation of the body is the first foundation of mindfulness. It's a way of establishing a sense of presence, and helps us to understand and to let go of the desires, fears, and longings we can experience around the body.

The second foundation of mindfulness is contemplation of feeling. Of course, in English 'feeling' is often used as a synonym of 'emotion', but the Pali word for 'feeling', *vedana*, is not directly connected with emotion. *Vedana* simply means pleasant feelings, unpleasant feelings or feelings that are neutral, neither pleasant nor unpleasant. Some emotions are pleasant, and some emotions have unpleasant feeling, but *vedana*, the Pali word, is separate from emotion. It can refer to a pleasant bodily feeling just as much as a mental feeling -- both the body and the mind can have pleasant, unpleasant and neutral feelings.

Feeling is present in everything we experience, though usually we hardly notice it, we're not really conscious of it. All we know consciously is that we would like to have more of some things, and to get rid of others as quickly as possible, while with many things we never really notice them at all. So I find contemplation of feeling very useful as a foundation for mindfulness. It can help us to be more conscious of neutral feelings such as the feeling of clothing on the body, the feeling of air on the skin when it's not too hot or too cold, and also the times when we're not particularly bothered or upset about anything. These are all either bodily or mental experiences of neutral feeling.

I also find the contemplation of unpleasant feeling helpful: it helps me to react less strongly to the feeling. When I'm feeling bored, upset or confused, I tend to struggle with these states if I'm not mindful. But if I use the contemplation of *vedana* - recognising boredom or confusion as an unpleasant feeling - just noticing that this is an unpleasant feeling can help me to stay present with the feeling. The amazing thing is that when we're present with unpleasant feeling, it changes by itself. We don't have to struggle with it to try to make it change. In fact, struggling often makes it much, much worse, while if we're just present with it, it will cease of its own accord.

Contemplating unpleasant feelings in the body is also useful, because we tend to react instinctively to such feelings. Sometimes, though, it's helpful just to stop and recognise that okay, these are unpleasant feelings, and practise simply watching them and seeing them change. It can be very interesting if, say, you have an itch while meditating; if you can bear it, and just stay present with it, you can notice how it changes. I've found that sometimes if I stay present with an itch in one part of the body, it disappears from that part and then I get another itch somewhere else - it can be quite amusing!

However, we may need to respond more actively to some other types of bodily unpleasant feeling. For instance, if we have strong pain in the knees, sometimes just relaxing around the pain allows it to change and even to stop altogether, but sometimes we might need to change position so as to avoid causing damage. If we're sick we might need to take medicine. If the room where we're meditating is too cold or too hot, it's sometimes appropriate just to bear with it, but sometimes it's appropriate to put on more clothes or to open a window. But it's important to establish mindfulness before doing any of these things. In this way, we respond with wisdom and compassion, rather than just reaching out for something that may bring temporary relief, but which might, in the longer term, make matters much worse. I'm thinking particularly here of how sometimes people use drugs or alcohol to deal with unpleasant feelings. These don't really solve anything – instead, they are likely to lead to more serious difficulties.

The third foundation is the mind itself. Sometimes I liken the mind to a room. We have a room, a space, and when it's dark outside the room is in darkness. When the sun is shining outside the room it's quite light; it may be full of people at some times, but not at others. In the same way the mind is like a container that is affected by different things. It's affected by our moods, by the thoughts that we're having, and by our experiences. So in the contemplation of mind, we're asked to be aware of the mind when it's at ease, when it's in a relaxed and expanded state, and when it's contracted. You may have noticed that sometimes when you feel very good there's a sensation of expansiveness in your mind, but if somebody says something unkind to you or disagrees with you, the mind immediately contracts – it becomes very, very small and tight. This is just what happens; it's just what minds do, nothing personal. So this is an approach to contemplating mind or consciousness.

The fourth foundation is *dhamma*, which is not the same as Dhamma as a refuge, the truth. But like the word *nibbana*, which simply means 'cool' – as when a fire is extinguished - *dhamma* also has a very ordinary, mundane meaning. It can just mean 'thing' or 'object'. So this foundation refers to contemplating mind objects, the kind of things or *dhamma* that are happening in the mind. For example, we can contemplate the thoughts that we're having, or examine our state of mind in terms of what are called the Five Hindrances, noticing whether they are present or absent. The Five Hindrances, as I have said before, are sensual desire, ill-will or hatred, sloth and torpor, restlessness and agitation, and doubt. When we're troubled by a hindrance, sometimes simply noticing and naming it helps us to stop struggling with it. This is a way of establishing mindfulness of that particular mind object. We can also use the contemplation of mind objects to reflect on aspects of the teachings and how they apply to our situation.

So the first foundation of mindfulness is form or the body (*kayanupassana*). The second is feeling (*vedananupassana*). The third is the mind or consciousness (*cittanupassana*), and the fourth is mind objects (*dhammanupassana*).

# WORKING WITH
## OBSTACLES

A couple of days ago when I went walking in the forest, a huge tree had fallen across the pathway so it was very difficult to walk. This morning I went again and I was very pleased that a tractor had come and removed the tree. I was able to walk further into the forest. It is like that with our minds in practice. Occasionally there is a very big obstacle, a very big problem, and we may need to call in the professionals – sometimes people find that having psychotherapy or using some special technique can help them to work with a particular difficulty. However, during a retreat we usually work with smaller obstacles, and some of them just disappear on their own; with kindly attention, acceptance and being very patient, things can change. Sometimes change happens with just a slight shift in attitude. Frequently, too, there are things we can do as a deliberate strategy, so that either the obstacle is removed altogether, or at least we can work with it in a more positive way. I'd like to share some of the Buddha's advice about working with different obstacles.

If there is a particular mood of negativity towards someone or some situation, one thing that the Buddha suggested was that we replace it with a different attitude. It is very difficult to feel angry with somebody when you have taken time to consider what their situation is, what their intention might have been. Sometimes just putting ourselves in the other person's shoes can help us to let go of any anger or negativity that we might have towards them. This is a kind of *metta* or loving-kindness practice; it can also be helpful if we are feeling frustrated and upset about our own practice or things that are going on in our minds. Maybe we have a habit of being very harsh and critical of ourselves, and so we can experiment. Instead we can try being kind, understanding, and encouraging. This is something that I have found very helpful.

It took a long time before I realised how critical I am of myself. So one time, I made a New Year resolution to give up self-disparagement. I would give up being critical and thinking badly about myself. That was very helpful, because I had never realised just how much I criticised myself. I had plenty of opportunity to practise. As soon as I noticed a thought like, 'You didn't do that very well,' I would deliberately think, 'No. Don't go there. Don't think like that.' Of course, I had to do this over and over again, but it was amazing how, after just a week or two, I began to feel much happier and much lighter.

So we have to patiently recognise negative or hostile thinking. Sometimes people come to me during a retreat and say, 'Oh, this is terrible. I never realised how negative and hostile I was.' So then I say, 'Don't worry, in fact that's really wonderful - because having recognised it, now you can do something about it.' This is what the Buddha meant by replacing one kind of thought with the opposite thought. The simile he used for this was of a carpenter who uses a smaller peg to knock a bigger peg out of a piece of wood. Maybe this won't make sense to anyone who is not a carpenter - the idea is that both pegs can't be in the same hole at the same time. So that is the first method that the Buddha recommended for dealing with an obstacle; and we can use it for any of the hindrances.

Another strategy the Buddha suggested was to really feel the unpleasantness of a negative mind-state. This might be something we recognise in ourselves if we are going through a really grumpy, complaining time; or it may be easier to see it in somebody else. Probably most of you know somebody who is always complaining about everything, who manages to see the negative aspect or the flaw in every situation. The Buddha encouraged us to contemplate how unpleasant it is to live in that way. I know for myself that when I've listened to those complaining voices in my own mind and really experienced what they feel like, I realise that I don't want to think like that for the rest of my life – and I can see that I don't need to think like that. The simile the Buddha used for this one is quite shocking. He said it is like a beautiful person wearing a necklace made of dog carcasses – quite unnecessary, and really repulsive. That may be a bit strong, but it can alert the mind to this kind of state, and the fact that we do have a choice as to whether or not we wear that necklace.

Another strategy is simply to set the mind on something else. A very obvious example is that if there is a lot of thinking in the mind, we come to the breath, or to the body. As I've already suggested, we can see the mind as like a room. The things and people in the room are like the thoughts, the mental objects. We can think, 'I like this one, and I don't like this one, and this one's okay.' We can be very busy sorting out which thoughts we like and which thoughts we don't like, but have you noticed something else about the room? What else is in it? Space... So instead of focusing on the objects, we can focus on the space around them. Sometimes when there is a lot of thinking, all we can see is the thinking; it is as though it occupies the whole mind. But there is a way of recognising that the mind is much bigger than the thinking. Instead of focusing on the thought, we can focus on the space around the thought.

If we have a very strong emotion like anger or grief, we can start thinking about it and wondering what to do about it, thinking that something is wrong because we have it and wondering how to get rid of it. But this tends to make the emotion bigger and stronger. Sometimes it is helpful instead just to focus on the body. With emotions like anger, anxiety, fear or grief, there is always an accompanying physical sensation in the heart, the belly or the solar plexus. So rather than being caught up in the story, the event, or whatever it was that triggered the emotional reaction, we can just bring the awareness into the body and observe the changes as they happen in the body. That is a way of letting go. Rather than holding onto the emotion, being caught up or indulging in it, or struggling with it to get rid of it - instead of that, we let it go. In that way we can observe how it changes.

The fourth strategy is what we call slowing down the mental process. There may be a tremendous amount of thinking - perhaps the thinking is not all that clear, but there seems to be a lot of it. This strategy involves thinking much more deliberately; it's like bringing the thoughts to the forefront of the mind and having a careful look at what it is that we are actually thinking. Sometimes it can be helpful to write the thoughts down; at other times we can just play with them in our mind. If we are angry or upset, one of the interesting things we will probably notice is the thinking that is just a kind of mumbling in the mind. It is not very clearly articulated. So you can say to yourself, 'Okay, let's take a look and see what's really going on here. I want to hear what you are saying.' It's like a small child who's upset and just screams, 'waaaah!' – and you ask, 'What's the matter?' Often just doing that, and really attending to what is said, is enough to help the child let go.

The final technique, which the Buddha recommended only for very extreme situations, is forcible suppression. He said this is as if there are two wrestlers, one very big and the other smaller. The bigger one holds the smaller one down so that they can't move at all. Sometimes we may need to do this, but we can only do it for a short time because it takes a lot of energy.

For example, the emotion of anger might be so strong that we feel as if we might actually do something violent. Of course we're all practicing with the precepts, we've undertaken not to harm anybody, so when this happens we just have to stay very quiet and still, and strongly direct the mind to something else. Then, later on, when we have a quiet moment, it can be useful to take some time to consider why the emotion was so strong, why we were so upset. In this way we can gain some insight into the feeling of vulnerability, anxiety, or whatever it might be that brought about such a strong reaction, and perhaps find a way to avoid a similar situation arising again. But at the time the emotion can be so strong that we have to resort to this very extreme measure of forcible suppression.

I'm sure that all of you will have many more ways of working with the mind. These are just a few suggestions from the Buddha's teaching, and things that I've found useful.

## A GUIDED MEDITATION

Settle the mind. Settle the body.

Notice that you are thinking, and what you are thinking. If the mind is quite quiet, deliberately bring up some kind of thought - maybe think about what you had for breakfast or something like that, something quite neutral.

Be aware of the thought as a mental object, something in the mind that you can observe, that you can notice.

It may be that the thought seems to fill the mind. Now, I would like to encourage you to see if you can expand the mind a little bit, make it bigger. One way we can do this is by becoming aware of the room around us rather than just our own bodies. Allow the mind to extend out into the space of the room. See that when we do this there is very much more space around the thinking.

So we can focus on the thought itself, or we can put our awareness into the space around the thought. When we do this we will find that the mind is sometimes very involved with the thinking, but we can let go of those thoughts and expand the mind to create space around the thinking.

Spend time experimenting with being with the thinking, and then being with the space around the thinking.

## [PAUSE]

Now see if you can find one short sentence from the stream of thinking. If you find that difficult, just think up a sentence, a short sentence like, 'I am breathing,' or 'I like this practice,' or 'I don't like this practice.' That sentence can fill the mind, and we can create a space round the thinking.

We can also slow the thinking down. Take time to think each word, with a space before the next one. Whatever the phrase is, whether it is something that doesn't have much meaning or significance or something that is very emotionally charged, you can still experiment with it in this way.

If you find it difficult to listen to the thought you can visualise the words, making them big, making them small or making them different colours. If you have chosen colours for the words, you may find that the colours change as the intensity of the emotion or the thought begins to diminish.

As we bring the meditation to an end, I would like to suggest replacing whatever words we have in the mind with the words, 'May this being be well.' Just repeat these words a few times, allowing them to fill the mind and body.

# RECOLLECTING
# THE BUDDHA,
# THE DHAMMA AND
# THE SANGHA

It is useful to recollect the qualities of the Buddha, the Dhamma, the Sangha.

The Buddha is the one who is awake, alert, attentive to the way things are. The Buddha sees clearly into the nature of existence and is not deluded by the appearance of things. He knows the impermanence, the unsatisfactoriness and the impersonality of all conditioned things.

The teachings of the Buddha are referred to as the Dhamma. They point to the truth of our existence. Each one of us can realise this truth. Each one of us can know this truth for ourselves. We can use words, concepts and instructions to guide our awareness towards the tasting of truth. This is a direct experience. The Buddha said that the Dhamma was *sanditthiko, akaliko, ehipassiko, opanayiko*. These Pali words translate as "apparent here and now", "timeless", "encouraging investigation" and "leading inwards", wherever we are and at any time, we can taste the Dhamma.

The Buddha himself realised the Dhamma more than 2,500 years ago. He knew it directly for himself. He directed others so that they too could know it for themselves. Ordinary men and women were attracted by the Buddha and his teaching. They adopted the teaching and applied it in their own lives. Then they shared their understanding, the fruits of their practice, with others; they passed this understanding from generation to generation, right up to the present day. This is referred to as the Sangha, the community of the Buddha's disciples, They are described as those who practise well, who practise directly, who practise with understanding, who practise with integrity, who are sincere about their practice and who experience the results, the understanding that arises from practising and applying the teachings. We say that this Sangha brings great blessings. A simile that is often used is of a field, a field of blessings. The best kind of field is one where there is good soil, where we can plant seeds and take care of them so that they grow. The Sangha can be likened to good ground where seeds can take root.

In the context of a retreat, we clear the soil. We clear away unnecessary distractions through the practise of renunciation, or simplicity. We set aside our usual concerns and activities so that we can receive the seeds of Dhamma in a clear field; then through our efforts each day we take care of those seeds. We water them. We make sure that they have light and sunshine so that they can take root and grow in the fertile soil. In nature things grow in their own time, so we need to be rather patient. Having established the best possible conditions, we need to trust that that the seeds will take root and grow, and that we will be able to experience and appreciate their fruits. We need to make sure that we remove any weeds. We need to make sure that we protect the plants and take good care of them so that they can grow strong and healthy. During a retreat we cultivate positive mental attitudes. If we notice negative thoughts that may discourage and weaken our practice, we examine them closely so that we can remove them, and allow the plants to grow unobstructed by these harmful things.

Our practice is cultivating moment-by-moment awareness, noticing how things are right now, recognising how it is right now. If we feel negative, or full of greed, or dull and sleepy, restless or uncertain, we cultivate a friendly interest in these things. Then we apply ourselves to establishing and maintaining mindfulness, rather than being overwhelmed or struggling with these hindrances. With mindfulness we cut straight through to the truth of this moment - how things are right now.

So we can continue our practice using the breath as a focus, or if we're feeling very sleepy, maintain a strong awareness of the posture and if necessary open our eyes so we're fully alert, attentive like the Buddha; knowing that this is how it is right now, attentive to each moment.

# RIGHT INTENTION

QUESTION: Having noticed something, having accepted it, is that it? Or is there something else that we should be doing?

ANSWER: This is a question that relates very well to our meditation practice, and also to daily-life practice, how we live in the world.

The Buddha spoke about The Eightfold Path. There are eight different factors to this path – Right Thought, Right Intention, Right Action, Right Speech, Right Livelihood, Right Effort, Right Mindfulness and Right Concentration. Perhaps the factor that is most relevant to this question is Right Intention. If the intention is one of desire for sense pleasures, or aversion or cruelty, it's better not to follow that intention, whereas intentions to be generous, to be kind and compassionate, are wholesome intentions and it is good to follow them. The intention to liberate the heart is, of course, the best intention of all - to understand, to free the heart from suffering.

First I'll talk a little bit about Right Intention in the world. Then I'll talk about Right Intention in meditation. How we live our lives has an effect on our meditation.

I have always been interested in the fact that the whole of our monastic structure is founded on generosity. Monks and nuns could not exist if it were not for the generosity of lay people. The Buddha recognised that one of the greatest causes of human misery is selfishness, the desire to obtain more and more things and the fear of not having enough, or losing what we have. As soon as we start practising generosity, sharing what we have with others, we find that in fact there is always enough. We also discover that the heart is nourished in a quite particular way when we start to be generous.

In some Buddhist traditions they have a custom of putting a little of the food they receive to one side for the hungry ghosts. Once when I was living in the forest at Chithurst I decided to experiment with this practice and to share a little of my food each day with the animals in the forest. It was very interesting to notice the sense of pleasure that came from putting a little of each of the types of food to one side, even the things that I really liked. Even when there was less than I would have liked normally, it felt really good to share what I had.

There's a story from the time of the Buddha about a very wise lady called Visakha. Once she decided to invite the Buddha and the monks to a meal at her house. When the meal was ready she sent her maid to go and invite the monks to come. As the maid was going to the park where the monks were, there was a terrific rainstorm. The monks had taken off their robes and they were just standing in the rain, enjoying the rain falling on them. The maid came to the park and saw all these people standing there with no clothes on. She went back to Visakha and said, 'Sorry. I couldn't find the monks. There was just a group of naked ascetics.' Visakha realised what might have happened. She was very clever. By then, the rain had stopped, so she said, 'The rain has stopped, now go and invite them.'

Eventually the monks came to her house. After she had offered the food, she said to the Buddha, 'I'd like to ask eight special favours.' So the Buddha said, 'What would you like?' Visakha said, 'I'd like to be able to provide bathing cloths for the Sangha to wear, because nakedness is improper.' Then she went on to list other things that she wanted to offer, for instance special food for those who were sick and for those looking after them; food for those who were setting off on a journey and for those who had just arrived in the city; and a constant supply of rice gruel, which is a very pleasant medicinal food. There were eight requests in all.

The Buddha said, 'That's wonderful, but what benefit do you see for yourself in that?' Visakha said, 'Many monks and nuns come to this place, and when I hear that they have done well in their practice I shall feel pleased. I'll feel happy. When I'm happy my body will become relaxed. I'll experience a sense of ease and well-being. When I'm in a state of ease and well-being, my mind will become concentrated. That will support the arising of the enlightenment factors. These are the benefits I see.'

I find this an interesting story, because it shows that from something very simple like a generous action, there is a natural progression, leading to perfect liberation. A similar process is described when the Venerable Ananda asks the Buddha about the benefits of *sila* (morality). The Buddha's response was that because of *sila* there would be the absence of remorse; that would bring about a feeling of gladness - and then the same progression, step by step.

When we reflect on our lives, we realise we've all done things that are not so good. It's interesting to notice the way that the mind tends to be troubled when we have done something harmful or selfish. Conversely, when we have been able to avoid doing something harmful or selfish, or when we have done something good, we feel good about it - we feel glad. There is a very obvious connection between how we live our lives and how we feel about ourselves, and how we are in our meditation.

We are also encouraged to let go. If we have made a mistake, we are encouraged to learn from it and then to move on. We need to take care to avoid falling into the trap of feeling guilty and awful, and thinking that we are a terrible person. There is absolutely no benefit in that. It is much more important simply to recognise that we made a mistake, to consider what happened, and then try to be more mindful in the future. That is how we learn.

One of the misunderstandings about Buddhism is the sense that it is very passive; people assume that, as Buddhists, we just sit around and accept everything; that we don't make a problem about anything, but just make peace with it all. It is understandable how one could have this impression, but according to my understanding of the Buddha's teachings, and certainly looking at the example of the Buddha's own life, I can see that something different was intended. What the Buddha was pointing to was not that we should never react, but that our actions and speech should come from Right Understanding and Right Intention, from a wholesome intention. This is where accepting things first of all, and making peace with them is important.

We hear about so many things in the world that can make us angry and upset. We may feel we want to go out and change the world because we are so angry, but I'm not sure I would recommend that! However, when we consider deeply, we can come to a place of acceptance and understanding that these upsetting things are part of the human predicament. People do harmful things because they don't know any better. We may also see the harm they are doing to themselves. When we consider in this way our response is more compassionate. Perhaps then we can reflect on how we can help to change this awful situation. 'What can I do to help?' is a very different reaction from, 'I'm going to go out and sort them out! This is terrible, these things shouldn't happen!' A much better reaction is, 'This is terrible, how can I help people to understand and do things differently?' Then we can find many different things to do, depending on our own particular skills and interests. There are many different ways in which we can serve. So it's good to consider carefully in relation to things that we hear about - is there something that I can do?

It may be that in some situations there is nothing very obvious that we can do. If we visit somebody who is sick or dying, or somebody who is grieving, there may be nothing practical we can do to relieve their sorrow or pain. It may be that in those situations, just being able to accept and make peace with that feeling of helplessness, just being there with the person with a heart of peace, is the most helpful and compassionate action. Sometimes that is much more helpful than running around doing a lot of practical things, which may make us *feel* that we are doing something helpful, but which don't really have a very good effect if they're just arising from a place of inner agitation. As we practice our meditation and become more able to make peace with difficult emotions and feelings, we can contribute something much more subtle, much more profound.

So sometimes there are practical things we can do, sometimes there aren't, but just our presence can be supportive. It was interesting to notice the different ways in which people related to me when I was sick. At such times we tend to be more sensitive, so I could really feel if somebody was uncomfortable about my illness. The most helpful people were those who could just 'be' there, without necessarily saying or doing anything very much.

I was talking with somebody the other day about Right Speech, particularly in relation to something we see that is not right, that we feel is not as it should be; for example, if we feel that somebody is taking advantage of us or doing something that is not good. I was very grateful when I discovered the Buddha's advice in the scriptures about offering feedback. It was one of the things that I had a tendency to avoid if at all possible. But one aspect of our monastic training is learning how to be good friends to one another and, when necessary, offering some kind of feedback.

The Buddha said that there are several things we have to keep in mind when giving feedback. First of all we have to make sure that it is the right time. This means setting up the right kind of situation for the conversation you need to have. For me, the more serious the conversation has to be, the more care I take to create the right environment - to find a situation where we won't be interrupted and the other person won't be distracted. It's no good trying to tell somebody something if they're already upset, busy or doing something else. So we find a time when they can give us their full attention.

Then when we speak with them, we speak in a way that is gentle and kind, and from a heart of kindness - really wishing the best for them. This is very useful for helping them relax, so they can actually receive what we have to tell them. It's no good if they start to become defensive; they don't hear anything then. So we speak gently, with a heart of kindness. We also make sure we've got our facts right and speak clearly, giving them just the information that they need, not telling them a lot of extra things that may not be helpful.

These are the things the Buddha recommended keeping in mind in such situations. He didn't say we should never say anything, that we should never tell anybody anything that they might find difficult to hear. So if someone is doing something that is harmful and disruptive and causing a lot of problems, it's not simply a matter of 'letting go', putting up with harmful speech or behaviour; there are skilful ways in which we can respond. I find these principles very helpful, both in terms of interaction with another person, and in broader situations as well.

I was at a monastic conference recently where there were Buddhist monks and nuns from different traditions. As you are probably aware, the Theravada tradition tends to be quite conservative, particularly in the way that the monks and nuns relate to one another - the monks are senior, and the nuns are junior. There was some discussion about this and some people were expressing their concern about it. A very lovely monk who actually was very junior said, 'Well, if something's causing suffering, then it's good to do something about it!' That was very nice to hear. There was something so refreshingly sensible about it. Of course, it's not always quite so straightforward as that, but the whole idea that if something is causing suffering we should do something about it if we can is a very good example of Right Intention.

With regard to our meditation, the question here was whether just noticing and recognising a hindrance in the mind is enough. My response has to be that recognising it and accepting it is important as a first step. Whereas if we react from aversion we just make the hindrance bigger and stronger.

Years ago I used to have a problem with jealousy. Actually, it was more that I made it into a problem; because I disliked it so much I created a terrible problem out of it. If you have experienced jealousy in your lives, you will know what I'm talking about. It is so unpleasant that you don't really want to tell anybody about it. But it does have a powerful effect on how you relate to others; it's not easy to pretend that it's not there. So I had turned this jealousy into an enormous monster.

There is a story from the time of the Buddha about a monster, a *yakkha,* which is a kind of a demon. This *yakkha* went to one of the heavenly realms where Sakka, one of the high gods, had his throne. Sakka was not actually sitting on his throne at the time. He had gone somewhere else, but all the other beings and servants who looked after him were there. When the *yakkha* walked into the court they were all a bit shocked. So the *yakkha* swaggered in, went up to the throne and climbed up onto it. There was an uproar - 'How dare you! Get out of there!' But the *yakkha* just got bigger and bigger. Yakkhas love aversion and hatred - these are things that make them grow big and strong. So he was sitting there looking at everybody and feeling really grand. Then Sakka came back and saw what was happening. He heard the uproar, saw the demon sitting in the throne looking very pleased with himself, and like a gracious host Sakka walked up to the demon and smiled, and said, 'How good to see you. I'm so glad you're sitting on my throne. Are you comfortable? Can I get you a few more cushions? How about a cup of tea or nectar? What would you like?' At this point something rather strange happened to the demon. He began to shrink. He grew smaller and smaller, and more and more embarrassed and bashful. Then he slipped off the throne, bowed meekly to Sakka and left the court. The courtiers were amazed. They couldn't quite understand what had happened, but it had obviously done the trick.

So that was what I needed to do with the jealousy! Before I understood how to practise correctly, I used to make jealousy into a monster. I would see it as an enormous problem that I had to do something about, rather than simply seeing it as an impermanent condition that had arisen in the mind. I could definitely recognise it when it was there and it was clearly not a pleasant condition, but I didn't appreciate the fact that I didn't have to identify with it. All that was needed was simply to recognise when it was there, and allow it to change. It still comes sometimes - even now there are times when it pays a visit and I recognise it, but I don't make a problem about it, so it doesn't stay.

This I find a helpful story about accepting negative, difficult conditions that arise. Sometimes just accepting and recognising them is enough. It is a way of letting go of the aversion, the negativity. Ajahn Chah used to talk a lot about letting go. We may think that letting go means not having, or getting rid of something; but actually we can just *allow* it to go, rather than holding on to it or trying to throw it away. Like every other condition that we experience: if it arises, it will cease. And usually it ceases much more quickly if we can really let it go. Sometimes people use the expression 'just letting be'.

One reason I chose to talk about this was one of the other questions I received - a nice question which was, 'When we feel pain, tension, or itching, is it better to stay in the same position and observe it, or can we move and scratch?' I think my answer has to be - it depends. If you are on a retreat where the teacher says you have to stay still, then it's probably best to follow that advice. But I would say, 'Why not experiment? Try different strategies.' We can learn a lot from patiently observing an itch, but sometimes it is nice to get a little relief.

# BRAHMA VIHARAS

*May I abide in well-being, in freedom from affliction, in freedom from hostility, in freedom from ill-will, in freedom from anxiety, and may I maintain well-being in myself.*

*May everyone abide in well-being, in freedom from hostility, in freedom from ill-will, in freedom from anxiety, and may they maintain well-being in themselves.*

*May all beings be released from all suffering.*

*And may they not be parted from the good fortune they have attained.*

*When they act upon intention, all beings are the owners of their action and inherit its results. Their future is born from such action, companion to such action, and its results will be their home. All actions with intention, be they skilful or harmful – of such acts they will be the heirs.*

This chant is about what we call the Brahma Viharas: loving-kindness, compassion, sympathetic joy, and equanimity or serenity. The first section is wishing well to ourselves, and then wishing well to others. The second one is wishing that all beings may be free from suffering. Thirdly, may they not be parted from the good fortune they have attained, may they really enjoy the successes they have in their lives. And the fourth section is a reflection on *Kamma*, which can be very helpful when things happen in our lives. It enables us just to accept them for what they are, recognising that they are the result of what has gone before. We also realise that how we respond to things now will affect how things happen for us in the future.

# THE FIVE
# SPIRITUAL FACULTIES

One of the most important supports for the holy life, for the spiritual practice, is having good friends, spiritual friendship. So I think the hardest thing at the end of a retreat is when people have to leave, and return to a situation where perhaps there aren't people who share the same understanding and interest. Once the Venerable Ananda spoke to the Buddha about this quality of spiritual friendship. He said, 'This spiritual friendship is really marvellous. It must be at least half of the holy life.' The Buddha said, 'Not half, it is the whole of the holy life.' We need spiritual friendship to encourage us, support us and help us keep going in the right direction.

Some of you may practise together in groups or as a family, and that is something to be very glad about. However, even if you don't live close to other people who are practising, having spent this time together on retreat, you can now have a sense of connection with a broader network of people. It can also be helpful to think of the monasteries - the fact that there are monasteries in Britain and other parts of Europe. You may have had a chance to visit some of them. I hope everybody will have a chance to visit one or other of the monasteries in due course, because just knowing that there are people who have dedicated their whole lives to practising in this way can be a tremendous support to us.

I remember when I first went on retreat with Ajahn Sumedho and he had two or three other monks there with him. I saw them all sitting there in front of us with their shaven heads and their robes. They talked about their lives, and I thought, 'My goodness, if they're willing to go to such lengths – shaving their heads, wearing robes and keeping all those rules - there must be something in it.' The other thought I remember having at that time, having listened to Ajahn Sumedho speaking in a way that was so inspiring, was, 'But there's no way I could do that.' However, he then asked each of the monks who were sitting with him to give a short Dhamma talk – and at that point I thought, 'Well, if they can do it, I can do it.' That gave me the faith, the confidence, to carry on practising.

One of the things that I realised is important in my own practice is to support this sense of faith - faith that it is a practice worth doing, that it brings good results, and that I too have the capacity to practise and achieve these results. In the teaching on Dependent Origination, one of the links is that faith arises out of suffering. This might sound a little strange but, in a sense, it's obvious: we have to realise we are sick before we have any inclination to take medicine! If we realise that we are suffering, that we need help, then naturally we will be interested when we have an opportunity to hear teachings that encourage and inspire us; we will have the faith to pick up the teachings and apply them in our lives. This faculty of faith, *saddha,* is extremely important for us in our practice. It is one of the Five Spiritual Faculties that I will talk about this evening.

When you go on retreat you may think, 'Oh, I don't know if I'm going to be able to do this.' You don't have quite enough faith, and you may be tempted to leave. But if people come to me on a retreat and say, 'Oh, Sister Candasiri, I think I'm going to leave', I say, 'No, stay, you can do it!' I try to give them some encouragement to strengthen their confidence, so that there will be sufficient confidence and faith to support the arising of energy or *viriya,* which, as the second spiritual faculty, enables the putting forth of effort.

Just faith on its own is not enough. Faith is very important for setting us on the right track, but then we need to apply ourselves, to make an effort, *viriya.* A retreat calls for tremendous efforts: to come and sit for quite long periods of time, and then to do the walking practice; to get up early; practise restraint; keep silence, and so on. When we put in that kind of effort we are able to experience some of the good results of our practice, of our effort. Noticing those results increases our faith, and that makes us want to put in more effort!

The third faculty is mindfulness or *sati*. This means noticing and being aware of the movement of the mind and the changes in the body; becoming increasingly aware of our surroundings and other people, and generally becoming more sensitive, more tuned in to what's happening within and around us. With mindfulness we are also able to discern how to adjust our practice. We notice if we are feeling very dull or sleepy, and we stand up or open our eyes. If the situation is right we do some vigorous exercise. When we practise on our own we can experiment and find things that bring energy into our system. They will be different for each of us. Some of us will generate a lot of energy and inspiration from reading or study, or maybe from chanting - devotional chanting, or chanting mantras - or exercising, or talking with other people about practice or listening to talks and CDs, and so on. It is important for each of us to find out for ourselves what supports energy and enthusiasm for the practice.

It is also important to notice the ways in which we discourage ourselves. I've talked from time to time about self-disparagement, thinking badly about ourselves. This is something that can really take away our energy and enthusiasm. I'm very fortunate to have been a nun for so many years. I've never wanted *not* to be a nun, but I have been through times of feeling very discouraged about meditation, even allowing such thoughts as, 'I hate meditation.' But because I was a nun I stayed in the monastery, I had to meditate and I found a way through it.

We need to find ways to encourage ourselves and not be too demanding of ourselves, to be content with just attending to the mind and the body as it is. Saying, 'I have to have very strong *samadhi*, and I have to sit for three hours every day' is much too harsh and demanding. For some of us that may be helpful, but for most of us our practice has to be a much more modest undertaking. If we approach it in a more modest way, with a sense of gentleness, a sense of just feeling it out, we will grow to love the practice, and we will actually look forward to the opportunities to sit in meditation. And if we feel that we can't concentrate very well, we don't make a problem about it. Different people have different skills. For some people the mind concentrates very easily. For other people it doesn't concentrate so well, but they may have other important qualities; they may be very generous, or compassionate, or wise.

The next two spiritual faculties balance the first two. It's like a triangle with mindfulness at the apex. Mindfulness watches over and monitors how our practice is going.

The final two faculties are *samadhi* and *pañña*. *Samadhi* is often translated as 'concentration', but I prefer to use the word 'collectedness'. *Pañña* is discernment or wisdom. The sense of collectedness or *samadhi* balances energy. In our practice it is important to notice whether we are an energetic type who is always doing lots of things, or whether we are more into strong *samadhi* practice. I tend to be like the first type. I like to do things. I like to serve.

It is good to keep these two faculties in balance, both in our meditation practice and in our daily life, so that our activity is undertaken with a sense of mindfulness and consideration. We don't necessarily do a lot of things, just because we've got the energy to do them. We know how to pace ourselves. We need to balance times of meditation with times of activity, or times of rest with times of activity, so that we don't exhaust ourselves.

One of the interesting things about meditation, something that I've seen happen in different situations, is that it can make us very selfish, very preoccupied with our own practice. I remember many years ago, before I was a Buddhist nun, I was at a summer camp for spiritual practice in the mountains. There were people in the camp who loved to meditate, and they became very high and very refined, and very pure. They were so pure that they didn't want to do the washing up in case it upset their vibes in some way. But when we practise meditation we need to cultivate a sense of balance; not too much of one thing or the other. So our meditation informs our activity, and the sense of joy that arises from service supports our meditation.

With regard to the other pair, faith and discernment, we have all heard of the expression 'blind faith', where we carry on believing in something or doing a practice just because we've been told it is good for us. We have faith in that practice, or we have faith in the person who told us about it. There are some people who use the same technique of meditation for twenty or thirty years without ever really considering whether it is bringing any benefit or not. We need to balance our faith with intelligent consideration, with discernment. If we are not experiencing much benefit, we need to consider whether we are practising correctly.

There is a teaching that I very much like called the *Maha Mangala Sutta*, the Discourse on the Greatest Blessings. This discourse is a series of verses outlining all the things that bring blessings in our lives, which bring spiritual benefit. It begins, interestingly, with having wise friends, having good friends, and avoiding people who are foolish and deluded. So we really consider the people with whom we associate. Of course, if it is a close relative who is foolish and deluded it is probably good to spend some time with them, because maybe we can help them to see things more clearly.

As we practise, we gradually begin to realise that our interests have changed and so we are less interested in doing the things we used to enjoy. This can be quite painful, because it is as though some kind of change has happened, and so there is no longer a reason for being with some of the people we used to spend time with. However, of course, other people then come into our lives. We make new friends who have a similar interest, and can encourage us in what we really want to do.

That is the first verse of the *Maha Mangala Sutta*. Then it goes through many, apparently quite mundane things, like having a suitable kind of livelihood, cultivating beautiful speech (Right Speech), taking care of one's family, avoiding intoxicants, being patient, having opportunities to hear and practise Dhamma, and having insight into the Four Noble Truths.

I really like the final verse. It says, 'Though living in the world yet the heart remains unshaken. The heart does not tremble; it is free from sorrow, confusion or need.' I found this very exciting when I came across it, because it implies that there is the possibility of maintaining that sense of unshakeability of heart while living in the world. I had been on retreats and practised meditation, and I could certainly feel some degree of calm and unshakeability when I was on retreat. The suggestion that this might be possible even away from a retreat situation, even in the midst of a busy city, a difficult job or the impossible situations of one kind or another that we inevitably come across in our lives in this human realm, was very exciting to me.

One of the things people say when I ask them about their practice is, 'My meditation is still not very good, but I notice that now I don't get so upset by the things that happen in my daily life.' For me, when I began practising I was interested in the possibility of being less of a victim of my moods and more able to stay steady even when things are quite difficult, and everything is challenging me. This is what the Buddha could do; of course, all of us have a little way to go yet. But I find I'm very interested in the possibility of becoming stronger, and more able to stay steady when things are difficult.

Sometimes people think that living in a monastery must be very peaceful. They say, 'Oh, I'd love to come and stay with you in the monastery, with all those lovely monks and nuns.'

Well, certainly, the monks and nuns are lovely but all of us are human beings too, and we are all on a journey to liberation. When we live in community, there are times when we upset each other. When that happens we can't go to a pub and get drunk, or go to a disco and get it all out of our system that way. We just have to stay in the monastery, and we sit in the same place every day beside the same people. Sometimes we get along fine, and sometimes it's horrible; but we train ourselves to practise restraint so we avoid being abusive to each other, cultivating the quality of awareness that can stay steady. Whenever we fail, whenever we are not able to stay steady, whenever we become unbalanced or upset, that shows us where our next task is, where we need to put in more effort. It's like a fascinating game or a sport where we develop skill little by little.

So rather than feeling discouraged when we make a mistake, we become interested in it as a new challenge. We find ways to encourage ourselves and to maintain a sense of self-respect and dignity. It is a difficult path that we are all on, but it is a noble path. That is why we talk about the Four Noble Truths, because it takes a kind of courage to look into the real reasons why we suffer. It takes real integrity to face up to what might seem like weaknesses, failings or fears. We need to be very honest with ourselves - and many people aren't willing to be that honest.

Finally, to go over the Five Spiritual Faculties:

Faith (*saddha*) - faith that the practice is worth doing, that it is going to help us, to get us where we want to go. And equally important, if not more important, there is the faith that we have the capacity to do it, even though it might take quite a long time. I should add that we need quite a lot of patience as well.

Energy or effort (*viriya*) - when we have faith, we have energy. If we become discouraged our energy disappears. So it is really important to support faith in order to sustain the effort to apply ourselves to cultivating mindfulness, *sati*.

Mindfulness (*sati*) - *sati* watches over the other faculties and keeps them in balance.

Collectedness (*samadhi*) - this gathering and focusing of awareness is a balance to energy.

Wise discernment (*pañña*) – careful discrimination can be a balance to faith.

If we apply ourselves and keep practising and developing these faculties in a balanced way, we'll eventually come to the place where the heart does not tremble. We'll find that we can maintain this quality of present-moment awareness, no matter what is happening within us or around us.

# LOVE AND ATTACHMENT

The subject I would talk about now is 'Love and Attachment'. I think this is a very good topic, because quite often Buddhists understand or have a feeling that it is wrong to be attached and wrong to love people. There are even some really academic Buddhists who think you shouldn't feel any emotion at all. They pick up on the word 'dispassion' and think it means not feeling anything at all. So I find this theme of love and attachment interesting, because it's clear that people do love each other - I certainly love members of my family, and when I teach a retreat I gradually come to love all the participants. I develop a real concern and interest for their welfare.

There's a story from the life of the Buddha that I find helpful. Once, there was a rich, very influential merchant who lived where the Buddha was staying. The Buddha knew this man. One morning the man was out walking in the town, and he was in a state of great distress because his only son had just died. The Buddha's response to his distress may be shocking to some of you. He said, 'Loved ones bring sorrow.'

The merchant was angry; he didn't agree at all with what the Buddha had said. He went around asking people, 'Did you hear that? Did you hear what the Buddha said? He said loved ones bring sorrow. But that's not true at all. They bring joy. They bring gladness.' Soon everybody in the whole town was talking about this incident, and eventually word about the conversation even got to the palace, to King Pasenadi. As it happened, King Pasenadi's wife, Queen Mallika, was a very devoted disciple of the Buddha. The King and Queen talked about what the Buddha had said, and the King said, 'Do you think the Buddha really said that? Can that really be right?' The Queen said, 'Well, if the Buddha said it, then it must be true.' King Pasenadi was irritated by this. He said, 'If the Buddha says anything, you always say it must be true!' So the Queen decided to send a messenger to ask the Buddha about what he had said to the merchant. In due course word came back that this was in fact what the Buddha had said.

So the Queen thought about this, and then she went to her husband and said, ' I know everybody thinks that loved ones bring gladness and joy, but how would you feel if something happened to our beloved daughter?' The King said, 'Of course I'd be distressed if anything untoward happened to our lovely daughter, the Princess Vajiri.' Then the Queen went through all the people the King loved, and asked how he would feel if something happened to this one or to that one. Finally, the King understood what the Buddha was pointing to, and acknowledged that he was right after all.

Of course, if we love someone and there is a strong attachment to that person, we naturally feel sorrow when something bad happens to them, and if something good happens we feel glad. This is natural. This is normal. But as I said before, some Buddhists think that you should never be attached to people. I sometimes hear people say, 'I know I shouldn't be attached but I can't help it, I do love my mother a lot.'

We have a chant we recite quite frequently called *Five Subjects for Frequent Recollection*. It begins:

I am of the nature to age.
I am of the nature to sicken.
I am of the nature to die.
All that is mine, beloved and pleasing, will become otherwise, will become separated from me.

We could find these things incredibly depressing, but I prefer to consider this reflection as a way of developing wisdom and understanding. These are aspects of life that most people don't like to think about very much, but I've found in my own life, in my own practice, that keeping them in mind has actually helped me to appreciate things more fully. Whether it's an event or a relationship, this reflection has encouraged me to be very present and to treasure each moment.

As my parents were growing older I found myself dreading the time when they would die. I really didn't know how people managed to survive that kind of bereavement; so I would worry about the time in the future when they would die. But then I realised that I could perhaps spend my time more usefully by enjoying our relationship while they were alive, instead of worrying all the time about our inevitable separation. So I ended up having a good time with them. I made a point of saying things to them that seemed important, because I knew a time would come when I wouldn't be able to say those things to them in the same way. Then of course, when the time came for them to die, I did experience a lot of sorrow. I still feel sad sometimes when I think of them, and sometimes I wish that they were still here - but they were getting older and older and it was the right time for them to go. And I didn't mind the sorrow; I didn't suffer from it. There was just sorrow, and I saw the sorrow as the inevitable consequence of loving somebody. It's almost as though when you love somebody, there's a price tag attached. But I was very willing to pay the price. It wasn't too much.

So I would encourage you to learn how to love with awareness, rather than with blind attachment and the hidden demand: 'Please don't ever leave me. Please don't get old, don't get sick - and whatever you do, don't die!' Probably none of us actually thinks like that, but it's useful to consider what we expect in our relationships. Actually, it's not easy to love in a way that doesn't have a demand attached to it: 'I'll love you as long as you behave in the way that I would like you to behave, as long as you don't do anything to upset me.' We can put tremendous pressure on each other. It takes a lot of wisdom to be able to love someone and to still allow them to be fully and completely what they are - to let them follow their own path, their own journey.

I remember that when I decided to become a nun, I had in fact done plenty of things before that which my parents hadn't been very happy about - or wouldn't have been happy about if they had known about them. However, becoming a nun was something I did quite consciously; it felt like something that I needed to do. It seemed to be an important step in becoming my own person - liberating myself, and in some way liberating my parents too. In a way it was good that I hadn't realised just how upset they would be. I think it would have been very difficult to go ahead if I had known how much it would affect them. Obviously, I wasn't intending to upset them; I didn't want to upset them. What helped me carry through with the decision was encouragement from Ajahn Sumedho. He said, 'If you really want to help your parents (which of course I did), then become a nun and develop a bit of wisdom. Then you'll really have something to offer them.' In fact I think that was true, I think I was able to support them in ways that I wouldn't have been able to if I hadn't followed this path. And I was fortunate that even when I became a nun they still carried on loving me.

Groups of schoolchildren often come and visit Amaravati, because it's a good way for them to learn about Buddhism.

Sometimes the children are asked to write a report about their visit. One teacher sent us a copy of one of the children's essays about his visit. This boy was about eight years old, and I found it a remarkable piece of writing. One of the things that he commented on was a little saying that he had seen pinned up somewhere. The words were, 'If you love something, let it go. If it's yours, it will come back. If it doesn't come back, it never was yours anyway.' I find that quite a profound reflection. It was interesting that such a young boy actually noticed that and picked up on it.

One of the qualities of the Buddha that I like very much is a word that we recite as part of our morning and evening pujas. It's the word 'Sugato'. 'Gato' means 'gone', and the word 'su' means 'good' or 'well'. The way I understand this word is that it refers to the Buddha as 'one who goes well'; one who is able to live life fully and completely, and obviously very skilfully, and then to leave the past behind. I find this helpful because I notice that sometimes I can get a bit stuck in the past. If I make a mistake I can get stuck on it. My mind keeps going back and thinking about the mistake I made. It's interesting to notice the way the mind does that, how it tries to recreate, rewrite the past, rewrite a better version of the story, without that terrible mistake.

If I do something well, then again the mind can pick up on that, making much of it, blowing up the ego - 'What a wonderful person I am!' Once I heard a remark among a group of Dhamma teachers, describing this tendency to get stuck, to identify with something we've done: 'You're only as good as your last talk.' So even among Dhamma teachers there can be the tendency to get stuck on things they've done, either well or not so well. Whereas when we reflect on this quality of the Buddha, the *Sugato*, we realise that he did hundreds, thousands, millions of very good things in his life - he gave sublime Dhamma teachings, he comforted people who were grieving, and did many other wonderful things, but he was able to do them and then move on through life. What he did point to was that he was enlightened; my sense is that this was to encourage people to have faith and confidence in him - the kind of faith that would enable them to apply the teachings that he gave in their own lives.

So this epithet, *Sugato*, is something that we can contemplate. It's not that we shouldn't reflect on things that have happened, learn from our mistakes, and celebrate the things that we've done well - that's allowed. But we need to be very careful that we don't create a sense of self around this, either a hopeless, terrible self or the most wonderful, marvellous, sublime, incredible self - the 'better than everybody else' kind of self.

In fact the Buddha said that if we think we are better than somebody else, that is wrong view. If we think we are worse than somebody else, that is also wrong view. If we think we are the same as somebody else, that too is wrong view. Any thought of ourselves as a 'self', or any comparison with somebody else as a self, is wrong view.

So we can be aware of this tendency to create ourselves and to create each other. Of course, there's no doubt that we do exist in some way. We have these bodies. And we have minds. But if we really love and care about each other, we'll not create and fix each other as a personality. Through our practice of mindfulness we can meet each other afresh and allow one another to change, rather than holding on to an image of how we think they are or how we would like them to be. One of the things I have really appreciated about living in the monastic community, in the Sangha, has been living among people who have at least tried not to create one another.

So we try to avoid holding grudges, either holding on to an image of somebody as a person who makes a mistake, or creating ourselves as somebody who's made a mistake. If we are preparing to meet somebody, we can notice how we have an idea about the person and the conversation we are going to have. But I'd like to suggest adopting more of a 'don't know' attitude, so that our experience of being with the person is more direct, more immediate, rather than just meeting them through the idea that we have about them. We can see them as they really are in the moment, rather than through the image we have of them or a memory.

This is something we can experiment with as we cultivate this mindfulness practice. Are we able to let go of our images of one another? Are we able to allow others to be the way that they are, rather than holding them as a fixed image according to how we would like them to be, or how we think we need them to be? If we can do that, our life becomes much richer and more wonderful. It's almost as if instead of seeing something in black and white and one dimension, we suddenly see it in colour and in three dimensions. We still have ideas about people. We can still look forward to meeting somebody, or dread meeting somebody. We can look forward to a future event, or we can dread a future event. But we also have an opportunity to consider that, actually, we 'don't know', really we haven't a clue how it's going to be.

# MEETING DEATH

I was struck by the feeling of warmth that arose in my heart when I saw one of the group come back to the retreat. I noticed that other people looked quite happy too. This made me think that in some way, even though we haven't been talking to each other very much, something has happened among us during these days - a sense of community, like a family, has developed. So we felt a bit sad when somebody had to leave early, had to go away, we were concerned about whether they would be alright - and then, when they came back, we felt glad.

My sense is that when we practise together like this a lot happens among people, and mostly it happens in the silence - living together, getting up early, practising meditation, hearing teachings, and also attending to the very ordinary things that need to be attended to, just taking care of the place. I've noticed during these days a sense of appreciation for people's care - feeling really grateful for those who clean the toilets and bathrooms, take care of the rubbish, do the hoovering, and of course the people in the kitchen; and all the other ways in which we've taken care of each other, just quietly getting on with the things that we've been asked to do, or have volunteered to do. And of course this includes those who work with the computers, or telephoning, making lists and shopping - all those things.

It's as though something has been created through our living together like this; and even though it's just been for a very short time, it can be quite tangible. Of course, very soon there will probably be a different group of people sitting here - and most of us will have gone somewhere else. I find it interesting to contemplate the sense of gladness and joy when thinking about this time together - and then noticing too the slight sense of sorrow, a kind of longing in the heart, at the thought of separating. Sometimes we can think that this is wrong - that we shouldn't feel sad. If we were true Buddhists we would be completely dispassionate, there would be none of these untidy emotions that arise when we don't want them, and which we think shouldn't be there. But as I've said, my sense is that the Buddhist practice is actually a lot more subtle than simply not feeling things. When we talk about dispassion, letting go or equanimity, my own understanding is that it's much more about not minding what we feel, not struggling with it. If we're feeling glad and happy, we notice that. If we feel sorrow and grief, we notice that. If we feel really irritable and angry and confused, we notice that too, we allow that into consciousness.

When we're growing up we're generally taught about what it's okay to feel and what we shouldn't feel. For example, in Britain when children are growing up, boys tend to be told that they shouldn't cry. It's all right for girls to cry, but not boys, and certainly not for grown men to cry. We're also we're told that we shouldn't express anger - at least, that was part of my upbringing. And there are probably many other things that we're conditioned to believe are either okay or not okay, so we can become very skilled at repressing, just pushing down the things that are not okay; keeping them under tight control.

However, coming on a retreat is an opportunity for the mind and body to relax, so we can experience all kinds of things, even during a short retreat like this. I think we all need encouragement to not worry about any of it, but simply allow things into consciousness as a very natural process, and then to let them go. Some people call it 'brain-washing' - not in the usual sense in which that word is used - but more allowing ourselves to observe, to notice, all the repressed things as they arise in consciousness so that then we can let them go.

My sense is that during this retreat people have had a chance to experience quite a lot of calm. But some people also describe enormous amounts of thinking and remembering all kinds of different things. Sometimes people may experience grief that has been repressed, that they could never really allow themselves to experience at the time of the loss. These things may seem disturbing, but really they are quite all right. It's much better to have them up there in consciousness where we can know them for what they are rather than held down below the surface of consciousness.

Sometimes people think they are going crazy when they come on retreat; they have crazy thoughts and weird images arising in the mind. I always think of this as part of the general Spring-cleaning, and nothing at all to worry about. Some people ask about unusual body sensations, the heart beating very fast, or feelings of strange energies in the body. These too are things that can arise when the mind quietens down a bit, and again they're nothing to worry about. The only concern would be if they were so very pleasant that we became attached to them - and then spent the rest of our life trying to get them back again. That would be unfortunate. In meditation all kinds of things can arise: visions of light, or hearing unusual sounds or having strange bodily sensations. These are all just things to notice, to be aware that they've arisen, and noticing also their cessation. Some people experience such things, some people don't.

The cultivation of mindfulness, this way of establishing a strong sense of presence, is a very valuable cultivation. Some people do retreats simply so that they can experience the calm mind, and they attach great importance to that. But that sense of calm is dependent on quite particular conditions - long hours of meditation, external quiet, and all kinds of other very specific conditions that enable and support a sense of calm. While I have absolutely nothing against those experiences, it is clear to me that in some ways they are quite limited, because we can't spend the whole of our life living under such conditions. We have to interact with other people; even living in a monastery there's an enormous amount of interaction. Most people have jobs. Many people also have family responsibilities, and many live in situations where those around them are not particularly interested in meditation. And so we need to consider how the practice can be sustained in a meaningful way.

As I've already said, one of my absolutely favourite *suttas* is the Discourse on the Greatest Blessings. This was the Buddha's response to a *devata*, a heavenly being who came to visit him early one morning. It is said that this was the time of day that the Buddha used to give instructions to the *devatas*. So this particularly radiant being came and asked him what it is that brings most happiness. The Buddha listed quite a number of conditions; for example, associating with good people, having a suitable means of livelihood - something that doesn't involve any kind of dishonesty or harm, having respect for one's parents and caring for them if that's necessary, caring for one's family, keeping the Precepts, avoiding intoxication or unskilful behaviour, cultivating patience, gratitude and contentment, and contemplating the teachings. In the final verse, which is the one I really like, the Buddha says, 'Though living in the world, the heart does not tremble. It is free from sorrow, confusion, and need.'

I find it so inspiring that there is the possibility of maintaining a sense of stability in the world where we have to experience so many different things; good and wonderful things, but also very difficult things or terrible things that can shake the heart, agitating it or making it flutter or tremble. We call those things The Worldly Winds.[1] But we see that through mindfulness we do have the possibility to hold steady even when the strongest wind is blowing. Now, I don't think this means that we don't feel things - I hope not, anyway - but more that we can maintain a balanced perspective with what we are experiencing.

Years ago a little old lady lived with us whose name was Nanda. She was totally deaf. She had a big hearing aid, but we still had to shout very loudly for her to hear anything we said. She really loved the Dhamma, and was totally devoted to Ajahn Sumedho. When she first came to visit us in the nuns' cottage she was eighty-three years old; from then on she used to come and visit us very frequently. She would have come to live with us permanently, only she had a son to whom she was very attached. She didn't like his wife very much, and thought that she herself was the only person who could look after him properly. Towards the end of her life she became a kind of honorary nun. There was some question about whether we should shave her head; but she had very beautiful white curly hair and couldn't quite bring herself to do it. I think she was worried about what her son would think. So her big act of

---

1 *Loka-dhamma: Gain and loss, honour and dishonour, happiness and misery, praise and blame.*

renunciation was to shave her eyebrows. In the Thai tradition we have the custom of shaving our eyebrows as well as our head.

Anyway, I was very fond of Nanda, and I used to look after her and help her. Eventually she died – hers was the first corpse I ever saw. They dressed her up in pink and put her in a coffin; she didn't look at all like the person I knew. There was a big funeral service, and afterwards I was completely overwhelmed with sorrow. Ajahn Sumedho was there, and quite a few of the other monks and nuns, and there I was crying and crying - feeling quite ashamed of myself because I was sure it was not right for Buddhist nuns to be crying. But I couldn't help it. Then it stopped.

We had another old lady who lived with us. There are even more stories I could tell about her. I also experienced a lot of grief when she died, but I was more mindful by then. And whereas previously the idea of loss and grief had previously seemed to be something awful, a bad and unpleasant experience, when we had the funeral for this old lady my emotional experience was actually very beautiful. There were moments of great sorrow that would arise with small things, like seeing some object that had belonged to her – but there was also lots of fun. The funeral was a very joyful recollection of this person's life. There was a tremendous feeling of tenderness, and a sense of celebration as well.

We buried her at Amaravati. One of the monks had made her a coffin, and the nuns learned how to carry it. They practised with sacks of rice to start with, so they could learn how to lift it up, and then to carry it without dropping it. There happened to be some builders in the monastery at that time. They had a digger, so they kindly dug the grave for us, and each day the nuns would practise carrying the coffin, and lowering it down into the grave. I don't know what the builders made of it! Then we had the actual ceremony, and everyone joined in. Although I wasn't actually carrying the coffin, I was able to help lower it into the grave. We all threw flowers in, and little things we thought she might have liked. Then we picked up clods of earth and threw them in. There was something wonderful about the sheer physicality: the weight of the coffin, the handling of the earth, and performing this ritual, this ceremony - that was very helpful. It felt like an offering, and a way of dealing with all the emotion that was there. So it felt like an expression of love, and joy, and sorrow, all those things. In a community where people are mindful, are present, there was a tremendous sense of ease around the changing emotions, a sense that whatever was happening was completely all right.

I often think of our emotional life as being like the weather. In Britain we have a great variety of weather conditions - all in one day; wind and rain and storm, and then a sense of calm and bright sunshine, all in very rapid succession - it was very much like that on the day of Sister Uppala's funeral - in fact, with Sister Nanda's funeral it was the same.

After that I wasn't so afraid of bereavement or grief, while before I could never imagine how people could cope with losing somebody really close. Certainly it's not an easy experience, but I've found that when I can be present it is bearable. Also, it's really good to take care in our relationships with each other; it's important to try to resolve any differences, otherwise there can be a sense of regret when somebody close to us dies, a sense that we've missed an opportunity to make amends. In fact, there are ways that we still can, but it's much better to do it before we have to separate physically, if at all possible.

The Buddha strongly encourages us to contemplate our own death. This can be quite a frightening prospect, because most of us don't know what's going to happen. Of course, some people can remember previous existences and previous deaths, but most of us don't have that ability, so for us death is a complete unknown. All we can be certain of is that it's going to happen at some time. I find that a helpful contemplation is learning how to make peace with doubt, the sense of not knowing: 'Should I do this? Should I do that? Don't know...'

Most of us are addicted to certainty. We want to know. We want to know where we are and what's going to happen next. When we're on retreats, one of the things that's most difficult about the Noble Silence is that we can't get the kind of reassurance we're used to getting from each other. Someone might not look very happy, and we might assume that it's because of something we've done, but when we're not talking there's no way to check that out. So we can feel very uncertain. So we can recognise that sense of uncertainty and how uncomfortable it is in own our lives, and instead of trying as hard as we can to find certainty, we can take refuge in the

Buddha, in present moment awareness. Life then becomes rather exciting.

I imagine that the moment of death can be truly terrifying if we haven't learned how to make peace with the sense of not knowing what's going to happen next, if we haven't really made peace with that. But if we have, if we can be truly at ease simply with that sense of presence, I think that death can be tremendously exciting – stepping beyond into the unknown. Once I nearly died, and I realised that I could have died without even knowing that I'd died. From my perspective then, it all seemed like a complete non-event. But of course each case must be different, so really I don't know...

During this time of retreat we've had a chance to consider what is really important in life - to review our priorities and to consider how we want to live for the rest of our lives. Of course, I'm not expecting that we've necessarily come up with a detailed plan, but perhaps we have begun to appreciate the possibility of being fully present; actually present to experience life fully and completely, rather than living in a memory of the past or a dream about the future. Of course, we can reflect on events of the past. We can celebrate the wonderful things that have happened to us, or that we've been part of, and we can allow such thoughts to bring a joyful feeling into the heart. We can also learn from past mistakes. And of course there are times when we need to make some kind of a plan for the future, like how we are going to get back home from the retreat tomorrow. These are practical things that we need to think about, and then, having done that we can focus all our awareness on the here and now.

So if people ask me how they can best prepare themselves for death, my answer would have to be: cultivate mindfulness, presence, live carefully and responsibly, and make sure you enjoy your life. Make sure you do the things that are important to you, so that you don't reach the end and think, 'Oh, why didn't I do that?'

# NIBBANA

When we practise together for a while on retreat, things become quieter. There's more of a sense of stillness in the room. So we can see the effect of this kind of retreat structure on the mind. Things naturally begin to settle when we stop stimulating ourselves and we stop receiving so much stimulation. Of course there are still the internal processes of the mind, the thoughts, the memories that arise, but at least when we keep quiet and we're not watching TV or travelling around in a big city, the mind is less stirred up. Things begin to settle.

Somebody was asking a question about *Nibbana,* so I thought I might say a little bit about it. That's what we're all striving towards, so I suppose it's good to have an idea of where we're going. This is something the Buddha talked about a lot in different ways, and he used many different similes to point to the experience of *Nibbana.* Even the word itself is interesting, because it's a word that would have been used in quite an ordinary way in the time of the Buddha - it just means 'cool'. It was a word they would use when they were cooking, if they were cooking rice. Obviously, when rice is first cooked it is very hot. You can't really eat it when it's first cooked; you have to wait until it cools down a bit and then you can eat it. So *Nibbana* was the word they used to describe rice when it's cool enough to eat - a sense of coolness, a sense of ease.

There's a phrase that the Buddha uses quite frequently in the *suttas* when he's talking to his disciples. He says, 'Because of not understanding four things, both I and you have had to spend many lifetimes trudging this round of rebirth, have remained in *samsara*' - which is the realm of continual wandering in which we're always trying to find some comfort, some peace, some satisfaction. We may become comfortable for a while, but then we become uncomfortable again and we have to move; always moving on, always wandering and looking for something comfortable and peaceful. Or some people may look for some way to keep stimulated and always be searching for more exciting, wonderful, thrilling experiences. Sometimes you even find this in spiritual circles, people going to this retreat and that retreat, and this teacher and that teacher, and looking for the perfect monastery. Ajahn Chah used to tease his disciples by saying it was hopeless to search for the perfect monastery. It just doesn't exist. I think this is a tendency we can all recognise in our own minds. We're always moving, trying to find something better; trying to get rid of the things we don't like, trying to get hold of the things we do like.

The Buddha himself had very similar experiences in his life. As you know, he grew up in a very privileged environment. He was the son of a powerful ruler and his whole youth was spent in great comfort. Whenever he wanted anything he was given it. In fact his father wanted him to be completely satisfied with his life as a prince, because at the time of his birth there had been a prophesy that either this child would become a wonderful ruler, a very powerful and successful ruler, or he would become a Buddha, an enlightened being. And, like many fathers, his father wanted him to follow what *he* had done, to be a ruler, he didn't want him to follow a religious path. So he did everything he could to try to keep him satisfied, keep him happy. But then one day, the young Prince met what we refer to as The Four Heavenly Messengers.

Now, Buddhist messengers aren't like Christian angels, which are often depicted as very beautiful with fluffy wings. The Heavenly Messenger was an old person barely able to walk, not able to see or hear very well, with not many teeth, skin all wrinkled and hair falling out and grey; a very pathetic figure. The second was somebody very sick, in a filthy and revolting state, having diarrhoea and vomiting, obviously in a state of great discomfort, the body covered with sores. The Third Heavenly Messenger was a corpse in a funeral procession. If you have travelled in India and seen funeral processions, you'll know it can be quite a performance, with lots of beating of drums as the corpse is carried through the streets. When the young Prince saw these first three Heavenly Messengers he was deeply troubled. He asked his companion what they were, and his friend said, 'Well, that's an old person, that's a sick person, and that's a corpse, a dead person.' The Prince asked, 'Is that what happens to everybody?' The driver replied, 'Yes, everybody grows old, and sooner or later they die. And of course people fall sick.' So the Prince was very troubled by this, because it showed the emptiness and futility of all the values that he'd grown up with.

The Fourth Heavenly Messenger was a religious person sitting quietly, serene under a tree, obviously quite aware of what was going on and yet not troubled by it in the same way. This was what led the prince to leave the palace; it seemed clear to him that the only option was to follow a religious path, in order to make sense of what he'd seen. There were many religious seekers at that time; they would undertake the most austere ascetic practices - fasting for days and days and days, not lying down to sleep, meditating for many hours and generally depriving the body of everything pleasant in an effort to subdue the desires of the senses. So the Prince tried these, and he excelled at all of these practices. But eventually he became so weak he couldn't carry on. He realised too that he hadn't got any closer to what he was looking for; he had just become extremely weak and thin. Fortunately for us, somebody came and offered him some milk rice, which he accepted, and gradually he regained a bit of strength.

Then he remembered an experience in his childhood when his father had taken him to a ploughing festival. Because the adults were all involved in the ploughing festival, they left the child alone under a tree. He must have been about seven or eight years old. He sat down cross-legged under the tree and became aware of his breathing in a very easy, natural way. He sat there for many hours enjoying this experience. We can call this *jhana*, a state of absorption. Eventually the adults came back, and according to the story they found him sitting in the shadow of this tree. Because he'd been there for many hours the sun had moved, but according to the legend the shadow stayed over him.

As the Prince remembered this experience, he thought this was a kind of pleasure that was harmless, which was not connected with strong desire. And he realised that perhaps he shouldn't be afraid of such pleasant experiences, and that perhaps they could even help him in his quest. So he went back to his meditation with his body a little more nourished and healthy, and eventually he came to perfect understanding - the state of *Nibbana*. He stayed enjoying this pleasant state for quite a number of weeks, and eventually began to share his understanding with others. The way that he formulated it was as the Four Noble Truths. These are the four things that he said needed to be understood in order to be liberated from *samsara*, to get out of the realm of continuous wandering. These Noble Truths are *dukkha* or suffering, its cause, its cessation and the path to its cessation.

So, as the Buddha taught, we experience the cessation of suffering when we let go of desire: whether it be the desire for sense pleasure, the desire for being or the desire for non-being. Now, we can only really relinquish such desires when we appreciate the unsatisfactoriness of achieving them, when we fully understand that they can never properly satisfy us. This is because all conditions – even the most pleasant – are impermanent or *anicca*; furthermore, they are all *anatta*, there is no inherent selfhood in any condition of mind or body. I think that probably each one of us has probably had a little insight into that. Maybe that's what has brought us here - a sense that there must be something more to life than just getting what we want!

It's difficult to appreciate fully that there is no inherent selfhood in any condition of body or mind, because we have such a strong habit of identifying with the body, with the mind, our qualities, our strengths, our weaknesses, our character, our personality. So we're not so ready to let go of that identification; after all, we put an enormous amount of energy into creating and maintaining our 'selves'. But the Buddha's encouragement is to challenge that sense of identity; this becomes more relevant, more interesting, when we really come to appreciate the suffering that we cause ourselves through this habitual identification.

It's interesting that rather than referring to himself as 'me' the Buddha describes himself as the *Tathagata*, the 'thus gone' - or it might be 'thus come', it's not clear, but basically simply a being that exists. He certainly had a personality, he certainly had many gifts; he was an extremely skilled teacher and very compassionate, and he also had a good sense of humour - but these weren't qualities with which he identified in any way. There was just a sense of 'being', of knowing things as they are, awareness - not like us, who can be so very concerned about our appearance, or what we do well, or the mistakes that we've made. Our successes and failures matter a lot to us.

We also identify with our nationality, our gender, our age, our political affiliations, our family, our profession. There are so many labels that we attach to ourselves, ways in which we describe ourselves that have a conventional reality, but we also need to appreciate the ultimate reality of our existence, which is not identified with any of these things. When we're fully present, we don't think of ourselves as being a teacher, a monk or a nun, a doctor or a nurse, or whatever. There's just the experience of presence. But if somebody comes along and challenges us, criticises us, or even criticises somebody we're close to or love, we can become very angry and upset. This is because we've identified, we're attached in some way.

Now, I'm not saying this to make anybody feel bad about being attached. Often it's just a fact that we are attached. The main thing that is important to notice is that this causes suffering. So I encourage you to really take an interest in this, to try to notice the extent to which you are attached to different things and how painful that can be, because only then will you be truly motivated to try to let go.

The Buddha used many similes in pointing to different aspects of practice. There is a very lovely *sutta* where he talks about his teaching and way of practice as being like the ocean. He says that just as the ocean slopes very gently, in the same way the practice is quite gradual. Little by little we begin to notice that we're not getting so upset about things which used to upset us. He also said that just as the ocean has one taste, the taste of salt, so this way of practice has one taste, the taste of freedom. So I encourage you to keep investigating, to keep noticing the ways in which you create a sense of self - all the ideas you have about who you are, and what you have to do, and whether your practice is any good or not, and whether it will ever be any good - and just to ask: is this true? Is this how it is? Do I really have to believe these things?

In this way, little by little, the sense of selfhood is dissolved. As we begin to see the way we create it, we begin to appreciate the possibility of not doing that anymore, and instead to just move through life without clinging, without attachment. This is the experience of *Nibbana*, where there's no longer a reaching out and attaching to anything at all, where our life simply becomes a response out of a sense of compassion and clear seeing, clear understanding.

So for all of us there is still plenty of work to do, but I hope I have been able to give a little sense of what it is we are trying to do. Ajahn Chah used to ask people when they came to his monastery, 'Have you come here to die?' I think they were probably a bit shocked by this question, but what he was pointing to was the practice of dying before you die, allowing the sense of ego and the sense of selfhood to fall away so that we live in Dhamma rather than in selfish desire. I used to be puzzled when people spoke about not having any desire. I remember asking Ajahn Chah and Ajahn Sumedho (they were both there) whether it was wrong to be greedy for Dhamma. They asked if it caused me suffering. I said, 'no.' So we can see that there is a desire that leads to further suffering, but there is also a desire that leads to the end of suffering. I think we'd all like to end our suffering, wouldn't we? So that's a desire, and that's all right. The Pali expression for that is *dhamma-chanda*, enthusiasm for Dhamma, love of Dhamma.

# KEEP GOING

We have been practising together diligently under very good and supportive conditions, established to enable us to come to a place of calm - certainly, at least, a state of external calm. Some of you might still not feel so calm inside but just your willingness to be here, and to maintain noble silence, and to follow the routine, has been very supportive, very helpful. Although most of you don't know each other, maybe you have never even met before, yet you all share something very significant - this interest in practice, in waking up, in liberating the heart from suffering. So during this time we have had an opportunity to practise as a community, supporting each other in this way, and having spent this time together quietly, there is a sense of companionship.

The Buddha said that the most important thing for people when they start to practise is to have good friends. We need people who can encourage and support us, guide us. The first of the great blessings listed in the *Maha Mangala Sutta* is association with good people and staying away from those who lead us in the wrong direction, who encourage us to do things that are harmful to ourselves or others.

When I first came to Buddhist practice I was quite surprised at how much emphasis was put on virtue or *sila*, on the way that we live our lives. I had already been practising meditation for some time within other traditions, and somehow I had managed to separate meditation from the rest of my life. Meditation was something I did on certain evenings during the week, and at other times I did other things. But what struck me most about the way that the Buddha teaches was the encouragement to see the whole of our life as practice. How we live, how we speak, and how we act are all part of our practice.

When we look into our lives we see that this makes perfect sense. We begin to notice the effect on the mind of certain ways of speaking and acting. For example, if we gossip or say something cruel or unkind, if we speak in ways that are unskilful, this has a negative effect on the mind. And it works the other way too. If we're always thinking negatively or critically about ourselves or others, that tends to be reflected in how we speak. Similarly, with actions, if we do things that are helpful, supportive, and kind, that has a positive effect on the mind. We can see this as a kind of therapy. Sometimes when I'm feeling a bit depressed or miserable, I will deliberately do something kind. Maybe I'll tidy up some part of the monastery or give somebody a gift, and I always feel much better after that. Whereas if I deliberately do something that is a bit mean, or avoid doing certain things that I should do, while I may get a certain kind of satisfaction, in my heart I don't feel very good.

So it can be very helpful to reflect on the importance of how we live our lives. Sometimes when I became discouraged about my meditation, I would just reflect on the fact that even though I still wasn't very skilled at calming the mind, I could do plenty of other good things - I could still be generous and kind and patient. Then, as I cultivated more skilful habits in how I lived, I discovered a sense of wholeness or completeness in the heart, a sense of gladness, a sense of joy - and this actually supported my meditation.

There are several teachings where the Buddha is asked directly about the effects of generosity, *dana*, or the effects of keeping precepts, *sila*, and each time he speaks about this sense of gladness and joy that arises. He would also say that when we take care to avoid doing things that are harmful, we don't have to experience regret or remorse, and so the body can relax. There's a sense of bodily well-being as well as a sense of gladness and happiness. Then the mind collects, it calms down quite naturally. These are just the natural effects of living carefully, kindly, generously. And as the mind becomes calmer, more collected, we're able to observe more closely the way the mind and body work, so there is the arising of wisdom, or insight.

Some of you might recognise here the description of the Eightfold Path. The image that is often used to symbolise it is a wheel with eight spokes. Like a wheel, this Eightfold Path goes round in a circle. Here we have started with Right Speech, Right Action, and Right Livelihood. This leads quite naturally to Right Effort, Right Mindfulness and Right Concentration - the way that we collect, that we gather the mind, focus the mind. Then, as the mind calms down, we can see more clearly and there is the arising of Right Understanding and Right Intention, aspects of discernment and wisdom. We come to understand the way life works, the way the mind and body work together. We come to appreciate the effect of speech and action on our mind. So, quite naturally, there is the inclination to speak and act carefully, skilfully. So it goes round in a circle.

This Eightfold Path is what the Buddha referred to as the Middle Way, and the instruction given is that this is to be developed. Little by little it leads to understanding, and liberation from all suffering or struggle. It's interesting that in his very first sermon, the first teaching the Buddha gave, he points so directly to this Eightfold Path, this Middle Way. I'm always very grateful that it's spelled out so clearly, with such clear directions as to things that I can do in my own life. I'm also grateful that it's described as a gradual path, a gradual training. This is something really important for us all to realise – that it doesn't happen straightaway, we're not instantly liberated. It takes time. It takes effort and a lot of patience.

This is why we need good friends - to keep reminding us, to keep encouraging us. They don't necessarily do this by giving us Dhamma talks or even by saying anything in particular about how to live or to practise, but more through their example. I find that I learn much more from watching other people - how they practise, how they do things - than by what they say. So I learn by noticing when things have gone well, when someone behaves skilfully, and I'm encouraged and uplifted by that. In our monastic community we have a very clear hierarchy. People who have been ordained for a long time are senior, and the people who have been there a shorter time are junior; people who just visit are not in the hierarchy at all. However, I find that I can be encouraged and inspired by anybody, not just by the senior people, the teachers, but also by junior people and visitors. Not even just by Buddhists - I find gladness and joy in spending time with anybody who has made a commitment to Truth, as it is manifested in any tradition. I love good people!

So the Eightfold Path, the way leading to the cessation of suffering, is the fourth of the Noble Truths that the Buddha pointed to in his first sermon.

The First Noble Truth is that life as a human being is difficult. Some people think that Buddhism is very depressing because this First Noble Truth says simply, 'There is suffering' However, when I first heard this I thought, 'Thank goodness!' I really appreciated such a direct pointing to and acknowledgement of something that was so completely obvious to me in my human life. It was clear to me that even though sometimes life could be pretty perfect - sometimes I could have everything just the way I wanted - it would change. And of course there were often times when it wasn't just the way I wanted it. Physically, there would be discomfort - pain, hunger, being too cold, being too hot, being tired or having too much energy. It often wasn't 'just right'. With the mind it was even worse. There would be times when I would experience irritation, frustration, anger, sadness, depression, confusion, lack of confidence, jealousy. It's a long list, isn't it? And however much I didn't want those things, they would be there. I might enjoy life when they were not there, but then they would come back again. So hearing that suffering is a normal part of life, and that someone as wise as the Buddha was pointing this out, was a great relief.

The Buddha's instruction for this Noble Truth is that this suffering has to be understood. This was interesting. It had never occurred to me to try to understand the suffering I had experienced in my life. I was much more interested in getting rid of it as quickly as possible, or distracting myself from it. But the Buddha said quite clearly that suffering needs to be understood. Now, for me, the way of understanding something - and I imagine it's the same for you - is by examining it, being curious about it, taking an interest in it.

Considering the Second Noble Truth, we find a clue as to how to go about this because it points to the origin of suffering; that there is a reason why we suffer, why we struggle. Basically, it's because we are attached to wanting things to be other than the way they are. Firstly, we want to have delicious, beautiful, pleasant, wonderful experiences. Secondly, we want to avoid or get rid of anything we don't like. And finally, we want to exist - as a separate, fascinating 'somebody'. There is the sense of self, which is conditioned and maintained in being with great commitment, and yet which causes us tremendous problems.

When we come to the Third Noble Truth, we find that if we let go of these three kinds of desire, when we abandon them, we experience the cessation of suffering. Suffering ceases. We experience a sense of inner ease and peace; sometimes it's like the peace, the sense of calm that comes after a tremendous storm. Often when we're really struggling with something it can feel like a storm going on in the heart, and when we let go there is calm.

In this way of practice we need to be very honest with ourselves. For example, we may be struggling with something, and although we can pretend to everyone else that everything's fine, saying, 'Oh, I don't mind. It doesn't matter at all!' - with ourselves, we need to acknowledge that actually we *do* mind. We are unhappy. We are struggling with this condition. So it might seem a strange thing, a kind of the paradox in our practice, that in order to liberate the heart from struggle we need - first of all - to acknowledge that there is a struggle. When I first came across this teaching I remember enthusiastically saying to someone, 'Well, of course - everybody suffers.' And the person was absolutely shocked - as if I'd said something really terrible. However, I think that many people don't realise that they're struggling, that they're suffering. We can become very skilled at making everything 'all right' in a very superficial way.

These Truths are called 'Noble' because they call for a kind of integrity, an honesty, a willingness to really look at all the things which we're most frightened of - where we feel most vulnerable, confused, frightened. But then, having had the courage to look, we can experience the benefit that comes from really acknowledging and letting them go; and we experience a remarkable sort of freedom and lightness. I have to admit that I'm always rather grateful that I only have to be honest to myself; I don't have to tell anybody else about my struggles. I may have shared some of my struggles with you now on this retreat, as a way of encouraging you to look more deeply and more closely, but I can assure you that usually, at the actual time of some difficulty, I would never tell anybody! Most of my struggles have been very private, because it's too often painful to let anybody else know about them. We can barely tell ourselves; but when we do, it's well worth the effort.

So the First Noble Truth is that there is suffering; and this suffering needs to be understood.

The Second Noble Truth is that there is an origin to suffering, which is the attachment to desires; and these desires need to be abandoned.

The Third Noble Truth is that suffering ceases. When we abandon or let go of desire we realise the cessation of suffering; we have a direct experience of that peace after the storm.

And the Fourth Noble Truth is that there is a Way leading to the cessation of suffering; this Way, this Eightfold Path, needs to be developed.

So I offer these thoughts for your contemplation, and I encourage you to keep going. Having set your feet on the path, it's really important to keep going. Don't give up. Sometimes things will seem to be pleasant and to go very well; you'll really feel that you're making progress. At other times it may not feel as if it's going quite so well, and you may feel discouraged. But all the wise teachers over the ages have just said, 'Keep going'. Ajahn Chah used to talk about the 'earthworm practice'. Earthworms are rather simple creatures. They're not too concerned with whether they're at the beginning of the path, or towards the end, or making great progress at all. All they do is continue working with what's right in front of them, burrowing through the soil. So I really encourage you just to keep going – letting go, establishing peace with whatever may be happening, and eventually you'll come out the other side.

# ABOUT THE AUTHOR

AJAHN CANDASIRI was born in Scotland in 1947 and was brought up as a Christian. After university, she trained and worked as an occupational therapist, mainly in the field of mental illness. In 1977, an interest in meditation led her to meet Ajahn Sumedho, shortly after his arrival from Thailand. Inspired by his teachings and example, she began her monastic training at Chithurst as one of the first four Anagārikā.

Within the monastic community she has been actively involved in the evolution of the Nuns' vinaya training. She has guided many meditation retreats for lay people, and particularly enjoys teaching young people and participating in Christian/Buddhist dialogue.